MY LIFE IN AND OUT OF THE ROUGH

○ ○ ○ ○ ○ ○

MY LIFE IN AND OUT OF THE ROUGH

The Truth Behind All That Bull****

You Think You Know About Me

○ ○ ○ ○ ○ ○

JOHN DALY

WITH GLEN WAGGONER

HarperCollins*Publishers*

HarperCollins books may be purchased for educational, business, or sales promotional use. For information, please write: Special Markets Department, HarperCollins Publishers, 10 East 53rd Street, New York, NY 10022.

FIRST EDITION
Designed by Joseph Rutt
Printed on acid-free paper

Library of Congress Cataloging-in-Publication Data
is available upon request.

ISBN-10: 0-06-112062-6
ISBN-13: 978-0-06-112062-6

06 07 08 09 10 NMSG/RRD 10 9 8 7 6 5 4 3 2 1

My Family
God bless you all.

My Fans
You've always supported me. I owe you everything.

My Kids
Shynah, Sierra, Austin, Little John—my all-time favorite
foursome.

My Mom
I miss you.

CONTENTS

○ ○ ○ ○ ○ ○

"TOO MUCH AIN'T ENOUGH . . ."

That's a line from a fine old country-and-western song by Billy Joe Shaver—and not a half bad title for my life story.

You see, I haven't led what you'd call an ordinary life.

I've traveled to six continents—and won golf tournaments on five of them.

In my darker days, I had a few drinks, visited a few hospital ERs, and did time in a couple of rehab clinics.

I've beat up hotel rooms, houses, and cars.

I've gambled away a couple of fortunes.

I live on Diet Coke, Marlboro Lights, and the support of my fans.

I've weighed as much as 290 pounds—and lost as much as 65 in three months.

And I've been married four times.

I guess you could say I'm not exactly a poster boy for moderation.

But I also won two of golf's four majors before I turned 30. Only five other golfers in history have done that. You may have heard of them: Bobby Jones, Jack Nicklaus, Tom Watson,

Johnny Miller, and Tiger Woods. I am humbled and honored to be on that list.

Sometimes I wonder how I'm still standing, let alone chasing my third major. But you know what? I've always done it my way, and I think the best is still to come.

So I'm writing this book to tell the whole story, my story. The wins, the losses, and everything in between—without the bullshit.

This is me.

....

A lot of people live in the past. They get stuck in a negative life because all they do is wallow in the bad things they did. How is that going to help them tomorrow? My past ain't the greatest, but it ain't the worst. And I don't have any skeletons in the closet. They're all out. I got all my skeletons out. Everybody knows everything I've ever done. (Or you will after you finish this book.)

So you could be thinking right about now, why in the hell, if he really thinks people shouldn't live in the past, is Big John Daly writing a book about *his* past?

Good question.

My answer is that laying my life out this way, trying to see it as a whole thing instead of a bunch of disconnected memories, helps me get a grip on the present and try to build a future. So I'm writing this book in part to help me understand myself—and get ready for whatever life throws at me down the way.

But I'm also writing this book because I believe I owe it to you, my fans. You've always been there for me, and I want to strengthen the bond between us.

Throughout my career, you guys have been my lifeline, my

port in a storm, my best and most trustworthy connection to all that's good and strong and giving in the human spirit.

Without you fans, I'd be nothing—or maybe dead.

So if you've stood by me all these years, through good times and bad, and held out your hands to me, isn't it high time you hear straight from The Lion's mouth why I've done some of the things I've done, how I feel about things, and what I see around the bend?

I think it is. I know I owe you my life, so to me it follows that I owe you the true story of how I've lived it.

My mother, God rest her soul, used to tell me, "Champions come from the heart." Those are true words, words I've tried to live by. I'm proud that those words—my mother's legacy to me—are written above the door opening out onto the University of Arkansas football field, and that Razorback football players slap that sign to remind them of her message as they go out on the field.

Champions come from the heart.

MY LIFE IN AND OUT OF THE ROUGH

○ ○ ○ ○ ○ ○

○ ○ ○ ○ ○ ○

ONE

PLAYIN' THE TOUR AND LOVIN' LIFE

Back in the summer of 1991, my first year on the PGA Tour, I wasn't exactly what you'd call a household name in golf, unless you happened to spend a lot of time in my mother's household.

Finally, after three and a half years of scraping by on the minitours and the South Africa Tour following my decision to drop out of college and turn pro in 1987, and after four trips to the PGA Tour's brutal Qualifying School, I'd earned my Tour card for the 1991 season. By the beginning of August, I still hadn't won anything, but I'd made about $160,000 up to that time, so I was feeling okay. I wasn't tearing it up or anything, but I'd made a bunch of cuts, and I'd finished fourth at the Honda back in March and third in the Chattanooga Classic in July.

All year, word had been spreading a little about this redneck kid from Arkansas who could really let it fly but sometimes had to do some looking for it after it landed. So at tournaments I'd draw some fans around the tee to watch me hit driver. I never saw too many people along the fairways watching me hit my second shot, but that was okay. I knew I had some other clubs in my bag. Anyway, I'd wind up that year leading the PGA Tour in driving distance with just under 289 yards (288.9, if you're a stats freak). That would be good for about number 98 in 2005, and probably out of the top 100 in 2006. But back then, it was like 6 yards ahead of Greg Norman, who was number 2, and people were taking some notice.

Playin' the Tour and lovin' life—man, I was 25 years old, and I had the world by the tail!

· · · · · · · · · · · · · ·

As August rolled around, though, I hadn't made enough money to qualify for the PGA Championship at Crooked Stick Golf Club in Carmel, Indiana, which is just outside of Indianapolis. I was close enough to know that if I'd made a few more putts along the way, I'd be getting ready for my first practice round. But I was far enough back at ninth alternate to figure I had no chance in hell of getting in.

The week before, I'd played the Buick Open in Grand Blanc, Michigan, just outside of Flint, and I'd stunk up the place, missing the cut by a bunch. So I went back to Memphis, where I'd just closed on my first home and spent $32,000 I couldn't afford on a new BMW for Bettye, my fiancée.

I did pretty much what I always did when I was home. Practiced at Chickasaw Country Club. Hung out with what-ever buddies were around. Probably ate lunch at McDonald's. Maybe played some in the afternoon. Went home. Had a few drinks, no doubt. Nothing out of the ordinary.

I never once thought I had a prayer of playing in the PGA Championship. A couple of foursomes of guys would have to withdraw for me to get in. There was no way that was going to happen, not in a major.

But then a few guys dropped out for one reason or another, and every time one did, I'd get a call from Ken Anderson of the PGA of America to tell me that I'd moved up a notch. Nothing to get excited about. Then about five o'clock Wednesday afternoon, he called to say I was now third alternate. Still not likely I'd get in, he said, what with the tournament beginning in less than 24 hours.

Now, most Tour pros wouldn't walk across the street to watch somebody else play golf, but I decided to drive on up to Indianapolis to watch the PGA, to hang out, and—okay, I'll admit it—to have a few drinks with my buddy Fuzzy Zoeller.

Fuzzy had won the Masters in 1979 and the U.S. Open in 1984. He was a serious player. A major player. And he was just maybe the most popular guy on the PGA Tour. And I was—as I said—not exactly a household name. Or put it another way: I was a nobody. But Fuzzy and I had met in 1989 at the Federal Express–St. Jude Classic in Memphis, where I lived. Being a local boy, I'd gotten a sponsor's exemption. Fuzzy spotted me and asked me to play a practice round with him. We've been close friends ever since.

But my best friend in those days was Jack Daniels. Had been since I was 19. Most of the time, I was drinking Jack like you wouldn't believe. A fifth a day, sometimes more. If I was in a bar, it would be Jack and Diet Coke. If I was home or in a hotel, I'd just drink it straight out of the bottle. Most people would be drunk for a month on what I'd had before dinner. I'd paid a couple of visits to emergency rooms in college to have my stomach pumped. But maybe the scariest time was in Falmouth, Maine, in 1990, the night before a Hogan Tour tournament began. I was partying with some guys, and I was having what had, over the summer, become my usual: triple Jack Daniels on the rocks, no water, three at a time. After a while the waitress said the bartender wouldn't serve me but one drink at a time. Fine. I'd order a drink, she'd bring it to me, and I'd drain the glass while she was standing there—and ask for another. After a little of that, I had to be taken to a hospital because I'd passed out with my eyes open and the guys I was drinking with thought I'd had a stroke or something. The next day I shot two under.

But none of that stopped me. I was still young enough and dumb enough to believe I was bulletproof.

Back then, JD and JD were quite a pair—practically inseparable.

....

Wednesday afternoon, my fiancée, Bettye, and I were on our way to Indiana. (Yeah, my clubs were in the trunk. That's my rule: never leave home without 'em.)

I didn't have a hotel booked, of course, but my agents, Bud Martin and John Mascatello, managed to get me a room that afternoon in a Residence Inn. I'd signed with John and Bud back in March after the Players Championship, and we used to laugh that the best move they made all that first year was booking me a cheap motel room.

I'd told the PGA office where I'd be staying, just in case, and when me and Bettye rolled into the Residence Inn at 2:30 in the morning and got to our room, the message light was blinking. It was Ken Anderson, the same guy who all week had been saying I wasn't going to get in. This time his message was different: "You're on the tee at 1:58 on Thursday."

Turns out the last three guys ahead of me on the alternates list had pulled out. Bill Sander was injured, Mark Lye didn't want to play without getting in a practice round, and Brad Bryant had an illness in the family. And then Nick Price withdrew because his wife was about to give birth to their first child.

So, thanks to Sue Price, I made it into the 1991 PGA Championship!

Happy as I was to get in, my expectations of doing much in the tournament weren't exactly what you'd call high. I hadn't been playing worth a damn, I hadn't played a practice round, and I was beat from being on the road for 10 hours. Didn't matter. I was just jumping out of my skin with excitement. I just wanted to go on out there and play the course.

Only one little problem: it was 2:30 in the morning.

Six hours later, after breakfast at McDonald's, I was raring to go. I had everything I needed—tee time, clubs, golf shoes, golf shirts, even a caddy, thanks also to Nick (and Sue) Price. When he found out on Wednesday morning that I was on the short list of guys still hoping for a miracle, Nick—who's one of the great guys on the Tour—called to wish me good luck. He asked if I'd consider using his caddy, Jeff (Squeeky) Medlen, if I did get in. Would I consider it? Squeeky was only one of the top loopers on the Tour at the time and a terrific guy to boot. You bet I'd consider it.

Where's the first tee?

. . . .

Squeeky and I hit it off right from the start. I'd never even seen Crooked Stick, but he knew it because he'd walked it in practice rounds with Nick earlier in the week. At 7,289 yards, Crooked Stick was the longest course ever to host a major, and my only strategy was to go out there and kill the fucking thing. Squeeky was down with that: not once did he advise me to play defensively or conservatively.

Squeeky was a damn good caddy—so experienced, so focused.

It was amazing how fast he got to know my game. He could club me right away, like we'd been working together for years. That's not easy. At the pro level, there are a lot of gradations. One guy's 8-iron is another guy's 7. One guy fades everything, another guy draws it. Low trajectory, high trajectory. And so on. That doesn't matter on your average Saturday morning, when most guys don't have caddies anyway. But for pros, it matters. A lot.

Right from the first tee, Squeeky saw how good I was hitting driver, and he didn't want any negative stuff—no backing down and playing safe and hitting the 3-wood—so he'd hand me the driver, and in that voice of his that got him his nickname, he'd say the same thing: "Kill it, John. Just kill it."

So that's what I did.

The first round, I shot 69—three under—which left me only two shots off the lead. Needless to say, I was pretty damned satisfied with that. Thinking back on it, the whole day was pretty cool: from ninth alternate to one of the leaders after the first round.

Thing is, though, I didn't know how near the top I was until the next day. Thursday afternoon was when that big storm blew through and the lightning killed a fan. PGA officials suspended play for a while at about 2:15, so our group didn't finish our first round. The next day they sent us out early to finish the last three holes on the back nine. That's why nobody knew about my 69—because it didn't get posted until Friday morning. No appearance at the media center, no having to face a bunch of cameras and a bunch of guys asking questions. Looking back, that was undoubtedly a good thing.

Thursday night, after grabbing dinner at McDonald's, Bettye and I went back to our motel room and hung out. Bettye played sports—she was a strong tennis player—so she understood competitiveness and had a good idea of what the day had meant to me. Me, I was just flat-out tired, as tired as I've ever been in my life.

But it was a good tired.

That first round, me and my playing partners, Bob Lohr and Billy Andrade, didn't have any kind of gallery following us from hole to hole. Mostly, the only people who saw us were folks just standing along the ropes, watching for big-name players as the groups came through. And anybody who did stay with our group had to be following Bob or Billy. Nobody was following me. Why would they? At least not at first.

Friday, though, when I shot 67 and got to eight under, it was a whole new ball game. I was leading the tournament! The PGA Championship! Me, John Patrick Daly, Tour rookie from Arkansas, I was the leader in the clubhouse midway through a major!

But you know what, because I hadn't finished my round on Thursday, I hadn't had all night to think about what going low in a major meant. I just went from finishing my first round on Friday to eating lunch to starting my second round, with not a lot of time to get all nervous about what was happening.

It's not hardly a big secret that one of the keys to my 69-67 start was my length. The first par 5 at Crooked Stick, number five, was the longest par 5 we played on the Tour that year. Still would be, I think, if we played it all the time—600 yards. Well, in the second round I hit driver, 1-iron to the middle of the green, and there I was, putting for eagle. Lohr and Andrade were looking at each other like, "No way he's on this green in two. No fucking way."

I guess I might have been a little surprised myself. I figured I'd get close, maybe up and down for birdie, but getting on in two and putting for eagle got me a little pumped. I two-putted for birdie. I'll take two-putt birdies any time.

Toward the end of Friday's round, some fan stuck his hand out as we walked from the green to the next tee box, and without thinking about it one way or another, I slapped him a high five. No big deal. It just seemed like the natural thing to do. But it caught on. Next thing you know, I'm high-fiving every hand I see. Now, Tour golfers aren't known for doing that sort of thing. Maybe they're afraid they might hurt their hands or something. I don't know exactly why I started, but once I did, I never stopped.

After the round, a couple of PGA officials grabbed me and took me to the media center. That was kinda cool. I'd been in the media center at Honda, but there was over a hundred people at Crooked Stick, all in the biggest tent I'd ever seen. Somebody asked me if I wanted something to drink. I thought about a beer, but I didn't know how that would go down, so I asked for a Diet Coke.

I don't remember much about my first time in front of the media that week. You always start with birdies and bogeys—that is, you go through hole by hole; you tell the reporters what you hit, why you missed this putt, that sort of thing. That's the standard routine, before they start asking questions about what you thought or what you felt or what you thought you felt. Golf reporters never see most of a golf tournament, at least not live. They only see what's playing on the TV feed in the media room. Some go out on the course, usually on Saturday, but even then they can only follow a couple of guys at a time. And there's 144 of us out there the first two days. So we have to tell them how we played, otherwise they wouldn't know. And nobody had any idea who I was, or what my game was like, so after they were finished with birdies and bogeys, there wasn't much anybody could ask except, "How'd it feel out there, John?" and "What do you think about the course?" and "How do you think you'll do tomorrow?"

How did I think I'd do tomorrow? Shit, I was still thinking about today.

Afterwards, my inner circle of buddies rallied around me and cheered me on. My best friend at the time, Donnie Crabtree, was there along with Rick Ross, who was sort of my coach. A few other guys from home, too. Mom and Dad watched it on TV at home. Fuzzy, the only Tour guy I knew well enough yet to call a friend, had missed the cut and hit the road, so I didn't hear from him until Saturday morning, when he called and told me to "go get 'em, keep on kickin' ass."

By the weekend, of course, I wasn't the mystery guest anymore. I have the tapes from CBS of that tournament, and I can't remember seeing any of my shots on Thursday. On Friday, I played early, so they weren't on the air yet. But by Saturday, things were nuts. The newspapers had been full of stories about me, and the galleries had caught on.

I was paired with Bruce Lietzke on Saturday; we were the last twosome to tee off. In the clubhouse after the round, Bruce had said to me, "I want to beat you, but if you keep on playing like this, nobody's going to beat you this week." Bruce is definitely a good guy.

On every hole now, I was high-fiving people, and after all that had been in the newspapers and on TV, the galleries were going wild. I mean, the crowds were yelling and screaming and hollering, "Kill it, Big John!" I guarantee you it was the first time I ever needed marshals and security guys to get from hole to hole. I was so happy and surprised and proud of all the people rooting for me, it started to feel like a big party, and it just kept getting bigger and bigger.

It all happened spontaneously. People were rooting like hell for me. I could hear it, I could feel it, and I guess I figured I would give them back something besides golf. If I went to

Crooked Stick and just hit the ball and didn't show them any love, maybe they wouldn't have taken to me like they did. Anyway, it was fun.

After only two days, I felt like I was their guy.

. . . .

The craziest thing about the whole weekend, in a way, was getting invited by Mr. Jim Irsay, owner of the Indianapolis Colts, to be his guest at their exhibition game on Saturday night. I didn't know this at the time, of course, but Mr. Irsay was a huge golf nut, and he'd seen the way the people in the gallery were carrying on, and so he had Mr. Michael Browning, the president of Crooked Stick, ask me if, after I got through with the media on Saturday, I'd come on out to the game. I said sure.

See, I love football. Love it. I don't care who's playing. I don't care if it's preseason or whatever. Just to see guys out there hitting each other, it's awesome. Hey, it's football—let's go!

It was a blast. I met all the guys in the locker room before the game—Eric Dickerson, Jeff George, guys I'd seen on TV. Got jerseys. Got autographs. Gave a few. Then, during the game, I sat in Mr. Irsay's box and signed programs for the Colts fans in the grandstand. It was great.

Next thing I know, I'm in the middle of the field at halftime, me and Bettye, with 48,000 people screaming their heads off after they introduced me. I mean, they were going nuts. I'd never seen a city embrace somebody like that, especially somebody they'd never even heard of three days earlier. All of a sudden, after what—72 hours?—I felt like I was the mayor of Indianapolis.

And I almost became something even better: a kicker in the NFL.

Before the game, just kidding around, I told Coach Ron Meyer and the Colts people that I'd been a field goal kicker in high school, so if they needed someone, let me know. Well, they told Mr. Irsay, and he jumped all over the idea. Right away, he was looking into having me suit up the following week and kick an actual extra point during the game. But because of the insurance issues—I could have been hurt or maybe hurt someone else—it didn't happen. Wouldn't that have been something? Who knows, maybe I missed my calling.

(I got another chance. That fall, the L.A. Rams—they were still there then—were playing the 49ers on *Monday Night Football*. Some PR guy hooked me up with the *Monday Night Football* crew, and that afternoon I hit a 3-iron out of Anaheim Stadium, where they were playing that night. Then I kicked a 35-yard field goal, barefooted. Don Meredith held for me. And John Madden put me on that year's All-Madden team. I got an All-Madden card! I was the field goal kicker on the 1992 All-Madden team!)

After the Colts game, me and Bettye went on back to the motel. I still had a lot of nervous energy, but I didn't have any trouble going to sleep, and I slept through the night. You know, looking back, I wonder why I wasn't more wired up or nervous or something, but I was just having too much damn fun.

. . . .

No doubt a lot of people figured I was going to piss it all away on Sunday. Can't blame 'em. I was a nobody. I wasn't even supposed to be there. It was just a matter of time before my nerves would get to me and I'd start spraying golf balls all over Indiana.

But I had something going for me that made me feel like, yes sir, I did belong. On Sunday morning, when I got to the clubhouse, I found a note in my locker.

Now, golfers aren't like baseball players, who'll typically spend a couple of hours in the clubhouse. Most Tour golfers go to a locker room to change their shoes, stash any gear they've brought with them, and check to make sure their flies are zipped. Really, that's about it. I mean, guys don't usually shower there, or get medical treatments, or sit around in whirlpools.

That's about it, as I said, except for one thing: checking their messages.

Things have changed a lot since cell phones and BlackBerrys came along, but 15 years ago, if an equipment rep or some friend of a friend looking to score tickets to the tournament or even your agent wanted to be sure to make a connection, the locker room attendant would leave a message in your locker. And if you're on the leaderboard on Sunday, you're going to find a lot of messages, even if you're some redneck rookie from Arkansas.

So there I was on the most important day of my life, trying to pretend I didn't have butterflies fighting to get out of my gut, reading a bunch of scraps of paper from all sorts of people who all of a sudden wanted to be my best friend, when I came on one, neatly folded, with the following handwritten line:

"Go get 'em, John."

Just those four words: "Go get 'em, John."
Nice note, but no big deal.

Except that it was signed "Jack Nicklaus."

Jack Nicklaus!

Holy shit! The guy I admired more than anybody else in golf, my childhood hero, Jack Nicklaus was giving me a pat on the back and telling me to go out there and get 'em. No way that didn't help me do what I did over the next 18 holes.

Even so, I still wasn't thinking consciously about winning or losing the tournament. Sounds funny, I guess, but I was just thinking about going out there and playing golf. Dr. Bob Rotella, a real smart man I got to know some years later, says that's called "staying in the moment," and it's what you're supposed to do. Get ahead of yourself, start thinking ahead to where you want to end up, and you're more likely to screw up and never get there.

Anyway, I wasn't scared. I had butterflies. But I wasn't scared. At least that's what I kept telling myself.

You wouldn't have thought it, though, by the way I hit my first shot of the day on Sunday. I hooked my driver into the trees, your classic nervous, anxious, what-the-fuck-am-I-doing-here overswing. But then I came back and made bogey, a helluva bogey, considering where I hit the drive. Made birdie on two, so I was par for the day and three strokes up on the field after two holes—man, I was in pretty good shape.

I was paired with Kenny Knox. Kenny wasn't particularly long, and I was outdriving him by 50 yards on some holes. That went over well with the fans, of course. On number eight, a 438-yard par 4, I hit driver and L-wedge, which tells you how far my tee balls were going.

I owned the par 5s that week: one eagle, 10 birdies, five pars, which comes to 12 under. On the other 56 holes, I was even par. I won the PGA Championship on the par 5s.

My second birdie on Sunday came on the fifth hole, that

humongous par 5 I told you about. Then, just when I started getting a little nervous about where I was and what I was doing, I ran off a solid string of seven straight pars. On the 13th, a par 3, I made a 25-footer from the fringe for birdie, and all of a sudden I've got my right fist going, waving it around big-time.

The 14th hole, a big old dogleg left, was a really long par 4, maybe the longest on the Tour, at 468 yards, but I was hitting L-wedge to it every day, and I had a birdie in the second round and three pars there to show for it.

At 17, a 230-yard par 3, I hit a bad 4-iron left into the bunker. The pin was cut about 5 feet from the left edge, so I should have played it to the fat part of the green. Anyway, I hit a sand wedge out about 20 feet, knocked it past about 7 feet, missed coming back, and finally tapped in for double bogey— and still had a three-stroke lead. You got to feel pretty good about your chances when you double-bogey the 71st hole in a golf tournament and still have a three-stroke lead.

Play it safe on the final hole and protect my lead?

No way: you gotta let the big dog eat.

Squeeky didn't hesitate. On the 18th tee, he handed me my driver without blinking an eye. The final hole was a par 4 with water down the right side. I figured, even if I hit it in the water, I could still make bogey and win. Well, I killed my driver smack down the middle and then hit an 8-iron from about 160 yards to inside 30 feet. That's when I began my "victory tour," walking tight up the middle of the 18th fairway, knowing I'd done it.

There were something like 35,000 people at Crooked Stick that day, and I felt like every one of them was on my side. For some reason, as I started walking, I began waving my right arm around, just like Arsenio Hall.

The hairs on my arms were sticking up, but I still rolled in a 4-foot par putt for a 276 total, three shots better than Bruce Lietzke.

The last guy to get into the PGA Championship finished first.

....

When I look at the tapes of the 1991 PGA, I see the same guy I am today, only a bunch of pounds lighter. I mean, my swing was in perfect balance. I wasn't hanging back. I wasn't de-accelerating through the ball. Hips turned good. I was making a full, strong follow-through on everything. Yeah, I'm more mature now. I don't push as hard as I did then. I don't get overanxious. And I don't let the dark side affect me the way I did back then—and later. But the swing and the game, they're the same.

I played fearless golf that weekend. I just went out there and hit the ball. I just did my thing. My short game was great: I hit my approaches close, and I made a bunch of putts from inside 10 feet. Most of the time the ball went where I wanted it to. When it didn't, I didn't get scared. I just went and found it and hit it again. I was fearless. That was the key.

(That, and Nick Price's wife going into labor.)

The very best thing about that weekend—aside from winning, of course—was the way the fans rallied around me. And they've been with me ever since. That Saturday night at the Colts game? It was like that at St. Andrews four years later when I won the British. It's like that in Houston, in San Diego, in Augusta, pretty much wherever I play—no matter how I'm playing at the time, no matter how much I've screwed up along the way.

And it all began 15 years ago in Indianapolis.

It all happened so fast. The whole week was a blur. I've thought about it a lot. I've answered a million questions about it. But except for the Colts game, it was just like every other tournament week: wake up, breakfast from McDonald's, play golf, dinner from McDonald's, go to bed, then wake up and do it all again. You'd figure with all that was going on, and with me seeing my name on the top of the leaderboard at a major, that I'd have trouble sleeping or something. Uh-uh. I slept like a baby every night.

The only difference was that on Sunday night when I went to sleep, I was the 1991 PGA champion.

○ ○ ○ ○ ○ ○

TWO

FINDING MY WAY HOME

I was born in Carmichael, California, near Sacramento, on April 28, 1966. I don't remember much about California, though, because when I was four years old, my father, Jim, moved my mother, Lou, my sister, Julia, my brother, Jamie, and me to Dardanelle, Arkansas.

That's where I learned to play golf.

Dad was a construction worker who helped build the Unit One nuclear power plant right outside Russellville, just on the other side of the Arkansas River from Dardanelle. Dad was always being yanked back and forth between the day shift and the night shift, and he was always being called away to work on some other plant in another state when they had an outage or something. Sometimes he'd be gone two months or so at a time. Then, when he came back, it seemed like he'd always be catching the night shift and sleeping days. My brother, sister, and I really didn't get to spend a lot of time with Dad when we were growing up.

Mom pretty much raised us. Everybody called her Momma Lou. She ran a pretty tight ship, mostly without ever having to raise her voice. When she did take a belt to me or Jamie, it was because we really needed it. She sewed a lot—she even made a lot of our school shirts—and she was a good cook. Even now, I can close my eyes and taste her chocolate gravy and hot biscuits. But my last couple of years in high school, she was gone a lot. She'd go off to Kansas City when my father was working up there. Later, when he got assigned to a plant in Beaver Falls, Pennsylvania, she'd go up there for three weeks at a pop, come back for a weekend, then go back again.

Mom died in November 2002. I miss her a lot. So does anybody who ever met her. Dad's still living in Dardanelle in a place I bought him and Mom near our old house.

Dardanelle's a town of about 5,000 people located right in the middle of the state—35 miles west of Little Rock, 75 miles east of Fort Smith, just south of the Ozarks. The Arkansas River runs through it. Russellville, on the other side of the river, has a population of about 35,000.

Our family wasn't rich or anything, but Dad always had work, and by the time I was a teenager, he was making decent money. He was tight, though. He didn't like to spend it. When Jamie or I wanted something, we always went to Mom. Or we'd go to Woodson's, this clothing store in Dardanelle, and we'd charge jeans, shoes, shirts, whatever. When Mom would see the bill, she wouldn't get mad or anything, but Dad, he'd sometimes have a shit-fit.

We were a close family, I guess, but in a kind of distant way. Dad wasn't around much. Mom was, until me and Jamie got to be teenagers, and then she started spending a lot of time with Dad when he was called away on some job. We never really talked about any problems we might have had. I guess we all sort of figured that if you had some kind of problem, you'd work it out by yourself. We kind of went our separate ways.

I know I never talked about my problems with anybody, except maybe Mr. Don Cline and Judge Van Taylor over at

Bay Ridge Golf Club, when I was a teenager. Seems like I was the one who was always asking everybody else if they were okay. I kind of let my own problems build up, I guess. If I was hurting inside about something, I kept it to myself.

Me and my brother Jamie were tight as ticks when we were growing up, even though we were real different. He was always working on cars and building things. I didn't have anything to do with any of that stuff. I was into sports. The only sport he cared about enough to do was waterskiing. He's 14 months older than me, and as teenagers, we always got along. But when we were little kids, we got into our fair share of fights, and it usually came down to a choice: get a whupping from Dad or put on the boxing gloves and fight it out in the backyard. We always went for the backyard.

Our house in Dardanelle was close to the Bay Ridge Country Club. Back then it was your basic country nine-hole track. It didn't even have a bunker at the time. But it's located on a great piece of property. From one point, on the fourth hole, you can see maybe 25 miles, all the way to Mount Nebo and Lake Arkansas. It's a beautiful place.

(Today, it's got 18 holes and a new name: Lion's Den Golf Club. I bought it in the fall of 2005.)

I got teased a lot when I was a teenager because of my size. I was chunky. Not really fat, but definitely chunky. Hell, I ate too much.

I loved Mom's fried chicken and mashed potatoes and hot biscuits, and I loved hamburgers and French fries and chocolate shakes.

I hated vegetables. I tried all of them, too, because Dad made me sit at the dinner table until I did. But every time I'd eat spinach or green beans or peas or any of that stuff, I'd go running to the bathroom and throw up.

I hated seafood, too. Even now, when I go to pro-am banquets at tournaments, they always have shrimp and salmon and lobster and crap like that, and I practically puke.

Other kids used to pick on me for playing golf. Back then, kids in rural Arkansas didn't play golf; it was an old man's sport. *Hey, Johnny, you're so fat you got to play golf!* I heard that a lot. I also got teased for these two big front teeth of mine. Even when I smiled, I tried to hide my teeth. I was embarrassed. Truth is, I wasn't much to look at.

We moved around a lot: Locust Grove, Virginia (between Culpeper and Fredericksburg), where I went to school from the seventh through the ninth grade; Zachary, Louisiana (near Baton Rouge), for the first semester of my sophomore year in high school; Jefferson City, Missouri, through the first half of my senior year; and then back to Dardanelle for the second half of my senior year, so I could graduate from high school there and qualify for in-state tuition at the University of Arkansas.

All I wanted to do as a kid was play sports. There's a picture of me at one of my first birthdays holding up one of my father's putters. The first time I swung a golf club—I was four and we were still in California—I hit a cut-down 7-iron about 30 yards on a beeline and smashed one of our living room windows. The first nine holes of golf I played at Bay Ridge—I think I was six, maybe seven—I shot 42. Of course, that was from the ladies' tees. My first score from the men's tees was 56.

That pretty much set the stage for everything that was to come. When we first got to Dardanelle, Dad played golf when he could, which wasn't all that often. But he liked the game, and we always had *Golf Digest* around the house, which played a major role in my golf education. We didn't belong to Bay

Ridge, but it was a semiprivate course, so Dad would take me to play with him from time to time.

That's pretty much where I grew up, if you want the truth of it. I spent so much time there, I guess you could call me Bay Ridge's unofficial mascot. Mom would drop me off after school, and I'd spend an hour or so wading in the pond, fishing out golf balls. I'd sell half of them to the club for spending money. The rest I'd put in my shag bag. Then, when I had a mess of 'em, I'd take Dad's driver over to the local Little League baseball park, which had three fields. And I'd find a free field and start hitting golf balls. At first, I'd just get up there and hit everything as hard as I could—that's how "grip it and rip it" got started.

When I was six, Dad bought me a used set of Jack Nicklaus MacGregors. Men's clubs. He once asked me if I wanted him to cut them down for me. I said, no, I liked them the way they were. That's why my swing's so long. When I'd swing one of those clubs back, the head would almost hit the ground.

(By the way, I played with those old Nicklaus MacGregors all the way through grade school until we moved to Virginia. There I got a set of used Spalding Executives. The first set of new clubs I ever owned was a set of Ben Hogan Directors that I won when I was in the ninth grade at a scramble, at Lake of the Woods, the golf course near where we lived in Virginia.)

From my first hacks with those old Nicklaus MacGregors, people have always tried to change my swing or weaken my grip or shorten my backswing or something. They'd tell me I'd never amount to anything as a golfer unless I did. I just wanted to prove 'em all wrong. When I was little, there wasn't really anybody around to teach me, and later, I didn't want to be taught.

A little later on, I started studying those old Jack Nicklaus instructional drawings that used to run in *Golf Digest*. I learned pretty much all the golf basics from those drawings—proper alignment, how to hold the club, that sort of thing. You could say that Jack Nicklaus himself taught me how to grip it, and that I picked up the rip it part on my own.

On the Little League ball field, once I got a little older, I'd set up at home plate, and I'd chip to first base, second base, and third base, and then I'd hit flop shots to the pitcher's mound, though I didn't know to call 'em flop shots at the time. Following those Nicklaus lessons, I taught myself how to hit a cut down the right-field line, a draw down the left-field line, and a straight shot to center. It was like having my own practice range.

The one sports lesson that Dad ever gave me—or at least the only one that I listened to—was to build up my left arm. When I played tennis, he had me shift my racket from right hand to left rather than hit a backhand. When I played Ping-Pong with him, we both played left-handed. He always told me to work on my left-handed shot in basketball. When I was nine years old, he had me hitting chip shots and putting with just my left hand. I've been doing stuff like that left-handed all my life, and it's helped. To this day, when I'm loosening up before a round in a tournament, I'll always hit a few chips and a few putts with just my left hand. And sometimes, when I'm practicing, I'll hit a couple of hundred one-handed wedges. That's the key to my short game.

As a general rule, they wouldn't let kids play at Bay Ridge unless an adult was with them, but sometimes I'd go out on Sundays and play the one o'clock scramble with Mr. Ken Brett or Judge Van Taylor or Mr. Don Cline. Funny, all the time I was growing up, I was comfortable being around adults. Most kids weren't. But adults seemed to accept me, and I enjoyed being around them—in part, no doubt, because I obviously loved golf and they could see I was good.

After a while, Mrs. Shirley Witherell, whose daughter Jane was the teaching pro at Bay Ridge, would sometimes haul me around in her electric cart, and we'd play 50 or 60 holes. Mrs. Witherell was a real sweet lady. Still is, as a matter of fact: she's in her 80s now, and I see her every now and then when I go back home.

As I got older, I started spending more and more time at Bay Ridge, hitting and chipping for hours and hours, always making sure to stay out of the way when somebody was playing through. My favorite practice place was on the fourth hole, which had this really wide fairway where I could practice hitting draws and fades.

Once, when I was maybe eight or nine years old, I said to Mrs. Witherell and Judge Taylor, "You know, one of these days I'm going to own this golf course." They kinda laughed about it, as you can imagine.

Well, the sale went through in August 2005. Yep, I bought my old golf course. Jamie, who has a construction business in Dardanelle, did a lot of work on it. It reopened this year as the Lion's Den Golf Club. Best real estate deal I ever did.

Until my junior year in high school, when I needed to be out there to be recruited, I never played in many junior tournaments, because we couldn't afford the entry fees and the travel expenses. But I'll always remember my first tournament, when I was 10. I shot an 89, and the kid I was playing against shot a 96. I kept his score, he kept mine, just the way we do on the PGA Tour. But the little bastard flat-out cheated: he said he "lost" my scorecard, and that I'd shot a 97. His father was running the tournament and naturally took his son's word over mine. Mom was really upset. So was I, but she was practically crying. I had to calm her down. I told her, "Never mind, Mom—he'll never make it, and I will someday."

(Turns out I was right.)

Those AJGA tournaments, when you get a little older—say, 15 or 16—are every bit as tense as the PGA Tour events. They're where college coaches come to do their recruiting. Play good and you could get a scholarship. Play bad and you better hope your parents have the money to put you through college.

When I was in 16 we were living in Jefferson City, and I heard about this AJGA tournament in Hudson, Ohio. We had cousins in Hudson, so if I could get in, we could stay with them. As I said, that was important because we couldn't afford a lot of traveling to golf tournaments. Back then, I think if you were from out of state you had to send a letter requesting to play. So I wrote this letter saying how much I wanted to play in their tournament, told them what my handicap was, and that I played out of Jefferson City Country Club, where our golf team practiced. All that. Usually parents write those kinds of letters, but I guess they thought it was kind of cool that I was taking care of my own business. Anyway, they let me in. Well, I ended up beating Billy Mayfair, who I now play with on the PGA Tour, to win the tournament.

The next year, I returned to Hudson as the defending champion. Like before, we stayed with our cousins. This time, though, I played just horrible. Dad was ragging on me pretty hard, really bitching at me because I'd played so bad. So I just left the house, right in the middle of this heavy rainstorm, and started walking. Walked for about an hour. It was a strange town to me, and I wasn't paying attention, and I got lost. Raining like hell, soaked to the bone, and I didn't have a clue where I was. Finally, Dad and my cousin, who'd been driving around looking for me, picked me up and took me home.

That same year, at the Junior World tournament in San Diego at Torrey Pines, I finished second behind Stuart Hendley. Make that, I would have finished second, except that I got a two-stroke penalty for grounding my club in a hazard, and finished sixth. We were staying with my aunt and uncle. When we got back to their place, I threw the sixth-place trophy on the ground and broke it. Mom got all over me. She asked me, "Did you do your best?" "Yes, m'am, I did, but I choked at the end." "But you did your best, John, so what do you have to complain about?" Mom always knew the right thing to say, even if I didn't understand that at the time.

Matter of fact, I don't think Mom's lesson ever sank in far enough. I've always had a tendency to brood about my game when I'm playing bad. Brood, and get really, really mad at myself. Sometimes I'll just kind of explode inside while I'm on the course. Sometimes I'll lose it altogether, just go haywire, and beat the shit out of a motel room or something.

Mom was right: if you do your best, try your hardest, then you don't have any cause to beat up on yourself. Mom was right, and I was wrong not to pay more attention to her.

My last junior tournament was the AJGA championship in Atlanta when I was 17. I probably shouldn't have even bothered playing in it, because I'd already decided I was going to Arkansas the following year, but I did, and it ended pretty ugly. The night before the final round, me and a few guys went out partying, and I got shit-faced drunk. The next morning, there I was, in the toilet stall at the golf course, puking my guts out. I barely made my tee time. I played just awful, and I stank to high heaven from the booze, so one of the officials pulled me aside to check me out, and he found a bottle of Jack Daniels in my golf bag. DQ on the spot.

Frankly, I didn't much give a shit, what with it being my last AJGA tournament and all, and I was there mainly to have a good time, and me and my buddies had seen to that. But my parents, they were really pissed off. They laid into me pretty good.

Growing up, I played baseball and football. In baseball, I was a pitcher (good speed, good curve, great knuckler). In football, I was a field goal kicker—and my senior year, I made all-state. My problem in sports was that I'm flat-footed and never could run for shit. I picked golf to focus on, but golf also sort of picked me.

School came easy. I never really studied, but I was a good listener in class, and I made A's and B's all the way through my junior year in high school. I was good at history, good at math, pretty good at English. But literature, I hated. I never liked to read, and I didn't see the point. Shakespeare sucked. I couldn't stand reading that shit.

I'm serious. I mean, you got to learn a little math, and you got to learn to read because you want to read the sports pages or a love letter. But what else is there to read?

Funny, though, I did like to write stuff. Essays and stories? Notes to friends? Letters? Fine, no problem. Today it's lyrics to songs. But reading about Hamlet or Macbeth or somebody like that to me was like, who . . . really . . . cares?

I never had a problem talking to people, making friends. Sure, all that moving from one place to another, it was a little tough sometimes. I'd make a few friends, maybe even hook up with a girlfriend, then—boom!—we'd move. But somehow it didn't bother me that much. As a kid, I always thought one of these days I'd be on the PGA Tour or playing in the NFL, and

I thought it was important to get to know people. Anyway, when I'd get to a new place, there was always golf, which I could do by myself.

I always played golf, whatever the season. When we lived in Virginia, we'd get some snow in the winters, and I'd be out there at Lake of the Woods scraping off the greens so I could practice my pitching and chipping. We had a dog named Poo-Poo. She'd go out there with me and fetch my balls. She'd always wait till a ball stopped rolling, then she'd pick it up and bring it back and drop it at my feet. Mom and Dad couldn't believe it. Tell you what, it beats hell out of having to go gather up your own balls.

As I said, we moved back to Dardanelle midway through my senior year so I could qualify for in-state tuition at the University of Arkansas. I'd gotten a half-scholarship offer that fall from Arkansas to play golf, and in-state tuition for the other half meant I could afford to go to college at the only place I'd ever wanted to.

Our house in Dardanelle was on 13 acres—nothing fancy, a log cabin, maybe 1,500 square feet, tops. But me and Jamie, who by then was going to school at Arkansas Tech in Russellville, we had it all to ourselves most of the time after we moved back, because Dad was off working in Beaver Falls, Pennsylvania, and Mom was usually with him. For better or worse, me and Jamie pretty much raised ourselves after our sister, Julia, got married and moved out when I was 14.

And let me tell you, me and Jamie used to have some mighty fine parties there. At first, we'd have about 20 or 30 kids from the high school on a pretty night. Jamie'd build a big bonfire out back on the property, and we'd all hang around it and drink beer. No big deal.

Then word started to spread, and pretty soon we'd get 200

or 300 people there. High school kids from surrounding towns, college kids from Arkansas Tech—shit, we'd empty out Dardanelle and Russellville and then some on a good Saturday night. Trucks, cars parked everywhere. Music blaring from radios and portable stereos, sometimes from local shit-kicking country rock bands. People drinking beer, dancing in the field, just hanging out. We had a trampoline in the backyard that we'd haul up next to the house, and then we'd all go up on the roof and jump off. It was about a 10-foot drop. We were all so shit-faced, it's a wonder somebody didn't kill themselves. I drank a lot of beer then, and whiskey, too. Truth is, I drank just about everything at those parties.

We always knew when Mom was coming back from Beaver Falls for one of her monthly drop-ins, so we always made sure the house was spic-and-span when she got there. I was your basic neat freak, even as a kid. (Still am, only more so.) I always had to have everything just so. So after we'd have one of our parties, I'd take care of the inside of the house, and Jamie would take care of the acreage, picking up all the beer bottles and trash. Mom never found out about those parties.

(Or if she did, she never said anything to me and Jamie.)

Like most kids, I used to sneak sips of Dad's beer, beginning when I was about eight. Unlike a lot of kids I know, I loved it. Just loved it. But the first time I got actually drunk was when I was about 12 or 13 years old. How it happened was that Dad used to make me and Jamie stamp on the grapes for his muscatel wine that he made down in the basement. He'd put it up in these big Mason jars and store it on shelves that lined the basement walls.

Well, this one time, we were mad at Dad because he'd made us stomp on these grapes for a couple of hours. I mean, we wanted to go do something, and we were tired, and our feet were all purple and blue and sticky. So Jamie and me decided we were going to drink us some of that wine. The next day, when Mom was out somewhere and Dad was at work, we drank a whole quart-size Mason jar between us. It tasted great, just like grape Kool-Aid. But we got drunk—boy, did we get drunk. I mean, we were drunker than Cooter Brown. We heard Mom pull up, and I hid in a cabinet underneath the kitchen counter. Jamie ran outside and hid in the backyard. But when Mom caught on to us, out came the belt. We were just lucky Dad wasn't there.

Every time Mom whipped us, trust me, we deserved it, and she always used a belt. But Dad, he'd use anything at hand—belt, stick, garden hose, whatever. And he hit hard.

Dad drank a lot of whiskey. A lot. And he was tough. He spanked us when we needed to be spanked, but he sometimes beat on us for no reason, too. When he got drunk, he could get pretty irate. I've seen him throw bottles at Mom. Before Mom died, she told us all the other things he did to her when we weren't around—beat her up, threw her around, shit like that.

Once when I was about 15 or 16, Dad was home, and he was out in the garage, where he'd often go to drink. I went out there to see how he was doing, and he said, don't worry about it, I'll get you a drink. So I had a couple of sips of his, and then he said, "Go in the kitchen and get me another Jack and Coke." He was already smashed. So I got him his drink, and I got me one, too, and I'm sitting there in the garage drinking with him and the next thing I know, he knocks the shit out of me and says, "Who said you could have a drink?" Dad could be mean when he was drunk, and he was drunk a lot back then.

But Dad wasn't always a bad guy. He also had his good points. He always encouraged me in sports. I took part in the Punt, Pass and Kick contest from ages 8 through 13 in

Dardanelle, and Dad painted yard lines on the street in front of our house, and would catch my kicks and punts. In 1974, I went to the Superdome in New Orleans to represent the Saints in the regionals of Punt, Pass and Kick, Eight-Year-Old Division. I got to the semifinals before some kid in Dallas beat me by 3 inches in the punt. The next year, I slipped while punting and nearly fell on my ass. I lost by about 6 inches. You could say I peaked in PPK before I turned 10.

Come baseball season, Dad would also play catch with me. And, of course, we played golf when he had time, but not so much after I started winning.

When Dad was sober, he was great. It was when he was drunk—and that was a lot of the time—that he was scary. I couldn't figure him out back then. Now I understand that he got just about exactly the way I got when I drank whiskey.

I guess you could say I pretty much learned to drink whiskey in high school, when me and Jamie would throw parties while Mom and Dad were gone.

One of the best parties, though, was one I gave myself the fall of my senior year at Helias High School in Jeff City. Mom was off with Dad in Beaver Falls. So me and Chris Hentges— he was later a great running back at Iowa State—and some of the other guys on the football team got together on Saturday night after a game. We had a friend, who was 21, get us some beer and some whiskey. People made a few telephone calls, and pretty soon there were 70 or 80 people at my house, all getting smashed. A bunch of 'em passed out and slept there all night.

Look, I want to make one thing clear—about this party and the other ones me and Jamie had after we moved back to Dardanelle for the second half of my senior year. We were rowdy, and we were loud, but we weren't violent or anything. We didn't trash anybody's property. We didn't wreck anybody's house. We didn't get in a lot of fights—a few, but not many. We just sat around and got drunk—and tried to get laid. Mostly, we just got drunk.

I think about those times and how much fun they were, and then I think about a lot of stuff that's happened since that hasn't been any fun at all, and then I focus in on July 4, 2002.

Me and my wife, Sherrie, and a bunch of friends were back in Dardanelle for a big Fourth of July cookout and party. It was a big party, maybe 50 or 60 people, with a lot of friends from all over. We threw it at my house, which is near our old place where we grew up. Me and Sherrie, we're staying in my tour bus, which was parked out front, and we're out there at about 10:30, when there's a knock on the door. It's Sherrie's friend, Kelly, and she wants to come in because my dad's been follow-ing her around, she says, trying to hit on her. Look—Kelly's 25, maybe 26, and Dad's 69. He's in his bathing suit, and he's drunker than shit. I tell him, "Dad, just get back on out of here, get back on out to the patio." Then I go get Jamie and tell him Dad's drunk, he can't walk, and we got to get him home.

Well, Jamie and I manage to walk Dad back to his house, and all of a sudden he bows up on me, like he's wanting to fight. He starts at me, and I just push him back into the chair. I tell him, "Dad, just sit down and shut up." Mom, meanwhile, is over at my house, listening to Johnny Lee sing—thank God, she didn't see or hear any of this.

After a while, Dad gets up and stumbles into his bedroom. We think he's going to bed. But all of a sudden he stumbles back out of the bedroom with a big old pistol in his hand, and points it at me, about 6 inches from my head. He was so ham-mered, he didn't know who the hell I was.

I'd had it with him. I say, "Just go ahead and shoot me—if

you don't recognize your own son, just go ahead and shoot me." You know, I think he might have done it, he was that shit-faced. But before he could, Jamie comes up, pushes his hand away, shoves his head up against the wall, takes the gun out of his hand, and shoots it off, I guess to get Dad's attention. Whatever, it worked. Dad looked up, and without a word, staggered off into his bedroom.

The next day Jamie talked to Mom and told her what happened. She was devastated. She really got up in Dad's face. He didn't remember anything. He had a total blackout of the whole thing. He apologized to Mom, to Jamie, to me, to everybody. All I know is that Dad was so drunk on Jack he didn't know who the hell we were, and that if Jamie hadn't been there, Dad might have shot me dead.

End of story.

Well, almost end of story. There's one more thing: Dad hasn't had a drink since that day.

. . . .

The reason I'm telling you this story now about my father pulling a gun on me is that, even though it only happened four years ago, I feel like it could have happened anytime while I was growing up.

Looking back, I can see that my relationship with Dad was complicated. There would be times when I wouldn't see him for months because he was off somewhere on a job, and there would be times when he was around that he supported me in my golf or whatever other sport I was involved in at the time. But there would also be times—a lot of times—that he'd be so crazy mean drunk that I just wanted to stay clear of him entirely, just to keep him from beating the shit out of me for no good reason.

Between those times and the times when Mom would be off with him, it'd be just me and Jamie and Julia at home—or later just me and Jamie. The only place I felt comfortable and safe was on a golf course. Anytime I was out on the golf course, it was just me, playing the game, even if I was playing with somebody else. And a lot of time it was just me, period. Late in the afternoon in Dardanelle or Locust Grove or Jeff City, hitting balls by myself until it was dark—and sometimes later, if there was a full moon.

Growing up, those were the most peaceful times in my life. And today, being on the golf course, inside those ropes at a tournament, clearing my head and focusing on one thing and one thing only—the shot I want to hit—that's about the only time and place I feel at peace from all the stuff that's rained down on my head the last 20 years.

The golf course is the only place where I feel really, truly at home.

○ ○ ○ ○ ○ ○

THREE

CHASING MY DREAM

Ever since my father taught me to holler "Ooooo, Pig! Soooie!," I'd been a huge Arkansas Razorbacks fan. Since we were first-graders, me and Donnie Crabtree would spend whole afternoons after school doing play-by-play of Arkansas-Texas football games. The Hogs always won, usually in the last few seconds, when me or Donnie would catch the winning touchdown pass or plow through a bunch of Longhorns into the end zone.

(Oh, yeah—we played in all those games, too.)

So now, going off to college to play golf for the Arkansas Razorbacks? Man, I figured I'd died and gone to heaven. Only better.

．．．．．．．．．．．．．．

If we'd stayed in Jeff City, I suppose I would have gone to the University of Missouri and played golf there, which wouldn't have been half bad. I'd won the Missouri Amateur when I was 16, so I had a reputation in the state. But it wouldn't have been the same.

Anyway, it turned out to be a great half year all around. Me and Jamie had the house pretty much all to ourselves while

Mom and Dad were off in Beaver Falls, Pennsylvania, where Dad was working at the time, and we were throwing all those hellacious parties. And all the while, I was getting more and more psyched about my dream coming true—playing for the Razorbacks, only this time for real.

The moral to this story is that you better be careful what you wish for. I went to Arkansas, all right, but I didn't play for the Razorbacks, at least not my freshman year.

See, our coach, Steve Loy, must have hated me.

Let me put that another way: Coach Loy *acted* like he hated me. Hell, I can't know what he really felt about me. I do know one thing for sure though: Steve Loy made me hate myself.

The day we all showed up for our first team meeting, Loy said to me, "You have to lose 60 pounds if you want to play for me." Period, end of story. At first, I was like, okay, he wants me to lose some weight, I'll lose some weight. At the time, I weighed about 235. Up some from the spring, when he recruited me—what the hell, I'd spent pretty much the whole summer drinking beer at the parties me and Jamie threw. But lose *60* pounds? No way. He had to be exaggerating to make his point.

But he was dead serious. And so I got serious, too.

At first, he had me on this bullshit diet of salad with no dressing and vegetables, which I hated, and fruit and nothing, absolutely nothing, fried. And he weighed me every day. I mean, shit, I grew up on my mother's fried chicken and her biscuits and chocolate gravy, and when I was a teenager I practically lived on hamburgers and fries. It didn't take long for me to come up with my own diet.

The first thing I did was change my drinking habits. Beer was mainly what had fattened me up over the summer, so I quit it altogether and switched over to Jack Daniels exclusively.

Pretty soon I was averaging a fifth a day, usually straight from the bottle—no glass, no ice, no water. I hardly ate anything.

Next I started smoking. I hated cigarettes, couldn't stand them. My mother smoked. It was the only thing I didn't like about her. Driving in a car, she'd keep the windows up so the smoke would be all around her. I hated that.

But Coach Loy said it would kill my appetite. And so I started smoking. Pretty soon I was up to three packs a day. I bumped up my drinking of Jack Daniels because I didn't want to eat the diet Coach Loy had me on: boiled chicken, a little bit of rice, dry salads, no burgers, that sort of thing. Oh, and I switched over to Special K for breakfast. I used to eat Frosted Flakes and all those sugar cereals, but I got used to the Special K. That was my best meal.

Coach Loy also made me switch from Coke to Diet Coke. That was tougher than learning to smoke: it must have been three weeks before I could get used to the taste.

Eventually, it got to the point I just wouldn't eat hardly anything. I'd just sit in my room and drink straight out of a Jack Daniels bottle, then go practice for three or four hours, come back, and start drinking.

Some of the guys got worried, but I wanted to play. If Coach Loy said I had to lose weight to play for him, fine, but I'd do it my way: cigarettes, a little dry popcorn, and plenty of JD. And the pounds were peeling away.

Then, one week late in October, I went something like three days without eating anything at all, and drank four fifths of Jack. I got the dry heaves and passed flat out in my room. Next thing I knew, I was coming to in a hospital in Fayetteville. It was my first visit to an ER with a whiskey overdose. I made another one later that fall. Of course, it wouldn't be my last.

But you know what? My cigarettes-popcorn-whiskey diet

worked. The pounds just peeled right off. By Christmas, I'd lost 65 pounds.

I probably ought to have written a diet book or something.

. . . .

I just couldn't figure Coach Loy out. I could understand why he wanted me to lose some weight, but he was always, always on me about it. Like when I left for Christmas break my freshman year, I was down to 172, but I came back 4 pounds heavier because I'd spent the break eating Mom's cooking. What'd he expect? It was the Christmas holidays.

Anyway, he said that's it, I wasn't playing until I got down to 170. Can you believe it? We hadn't even been walking the course yet because it was too cold even to practice outside, and he's worried because I'd gained 4 pounds over the holidays? Shit, being around Mom's chocolate gravy and her biscuits for 10 days, it's a wonder I hadn't put on 40.

Coach Loy was tough on all the guys, but he especially had it in for me. I mean, I was probably one of the hardest-working guys on the team. I practiced all the time. And all the guy could talk about was how much I weighed.

We had a dozen guys on the team, but only five could play in an NCAA tournament, with the best four scores counting for the team total. (Other tournaments, it might be six and five.) So if we had a tournament coming up, we had a qualifier—that is, the 12 guys would play 18 or 36 holes a day for two or three days. Stroke play. Theoretically, the five or six guys with the best scores would be picked for the tournament squad. Unless one of them was on the coach's shit-list for being too fat.

One time I'm leading by, God, I don't know how many shots. On the tee of this par 4, Coach Loy says to all of us as we come up to hit our drives, "If you hit it left, you're out of the tournament." (I guess he was trying to teach us something about course management or something. Nobody ever asked, and he never said.) Anyway, I'm trying to shoot the course record, and I don't want to set up for a fade and risk hitting it way out into the driving range on the right like everybody else. So I play my usual tee shot, a long draw, and it takes a bad bounce and kicks about a foot into the left rough. No problem. I knock it on the green and two-putt for my par. Meanwhile, the teammate I'm paired with blows it way right and ends up making six. And who do you think got picked for the tournament squad? Not the guy who missed breaking the course record by one shot.

My way or the highway—that was Coach Loy's coaching philosophy.

Another time, during a qualifier, my brain froze or something and I hit this really shit bunker shot. I mean, it was the kind of shot I'd been puring since I was 15, and I was steamed. So I threw my sand wedge towards my bag. Not good golf etiquette, I know, but no worse than you see a dozen times every Saturday and Sunday morning on every golf course in every state in the entire United States of America. Coach Loy didn't say anything. Instead, he picked up my club, and when I walked up to get it, he swung it hard against my right leg. Not a word, just this hellacious whack. I still have the scar on my shin to prove it.

That's what I took away from my freshman year under Coach Loy. A fifth-a-day drinking habit, a cigarette jones, and a fucking scar.

I got to play a lot my sophomore year, because two of our best guys, Mike Grob and Mike Schwartz, had finished school, Coach Loy didn't have much of a choice. We finished third in the Southwest Conference. I never won a college tournament. I finished second, third, and fourth a ton of times. I could have taken a lot more chances to try and win a tournament individually, but I wanted to make sure the team did good, so sometimes I wasn't as aggressive as I wanted to be. I was a good team player.

Coach Loy had us all playing scared. He had us in a "don't go for birdie because you might make bogey" mentality. We couldn't really show our talents. We were the probably longest-hitting golf team in golf in NCAA history. All of us could knock the shit out of it. But, he had this hand signal for 1-iron off the tee, another for 2-iron, and so on.

Let me just say, we hit a lot of irons off a lot of tees.

Bill Woodley took over in 1986 after Coach Loy left. They were as different as night and day. Totally different. We were all in shock. While Coach Loy only wanted things done his way, Coach Woodley let us play. Coach Loy was all about discipline. Coach Woodley was all about trying to win golf tournaments—how you did it was up to you.

Under Coach Woodley, we got to play to our strengths. My strength is hitting driver. The courses we played were generally pretty short, so I was driver, L-wedge on just about every par 4. And now, nobody was flashing hand signals telling me to hit 2-iron. As a team, we were a lot closer together and played a whole lot looser.

My junior year, golf became fun again.

We were closer as a team, but I didn't hang out with my teammates much off the course. Every now and then, we'd get together and shoot some pool or drink a few beers, but frankly I think some of the guys might have been a little scared to hang around me because of my partying ways.

You're not going to believe this, maybe, but I was a pretty

good student in college. My freshman year, I always went to class, paid good attention, and kept my GPA around 2.5. That tailed off some in my sophomore year, and in my junior year, when I was pretty sure I was going to quit and turn pro, I didn't go to class at all my second semester. But, hell, three years of college with a GPA safely over the 2.0 needed to retain his eligibility from somebody who hated school as much as I did? Not half bad, especially considering I didn't even buy books after my freshman year.

Like always, I was just plain bored by school. I stayed eligible, but that's about it. In college, just like in high school, it was, "Let's get to the weekend and party." Only the way I was drinking in college, it was kind of a party every night, even if I was sometimes the only one there.

I didn't know a lot of people. But once you got hold of a fake ID and got into a couple of bars, and the bartenders got to know you, it didn't matter whether you knew a lot of people. You can make a bunch of new friends every night.

Money was never a big problem. Don't get me wrong—we weren't rich or anything, and my folks sure weren't sending me any allowance. But for a long time I'd been able to pick up a little cash by scrambling. That's what we called it. Other people called it hustling. But whatever you call it, it was the same thing: playing other guys for money, usually men at the local golf clubs who thought they were better than they were, and who figured they could kick this fat kid's ass. That's the way I spent my summers (and a lot of weekends during the school year) when I needed a few bucks. Think of it as my permanent part-time job.

Remember, making my own spending money dates all the way back to wading in the pond for balls at Bay Ridge. Later, we always lived near a golf club in all the places we moved to. My parents made it clear to me: you stay out of trouble, and we'll get you close to a place to play golf. So I could always count on a little scrambling money to go along with what I made in my ball retrieval business. Plus, junior memberships at the clubs I played at were pretty cheap.

There's one chunk of change that to this day I do regret passing up. It wasn't until my sophomore year that I learned I could have collected $500 for incidental expenses—laundry and stuff like that—my freshman year as part of my half scholarship. Five hundred bucks! That would have been drinking money for a couple of months!

I'd been thinking for a while about not coming back for senior year, but I didn't make my final decision until early August. I called Coach Woodley and asked him if I was getting a full ride that fall, and he said, no, only a half scholarship, like before. That pissed me off, because some of the guys on full boats couldn't even qualify for a tournament squad. He said he was sorry, that if I'd come to him in the spring he could have done something about it, but that there was nothing he could do now. So I said, Coach, I understand, I should have talked to you earlier, but I believe I deserve a full ride, and I think what I'm going to do is leave school and turn pro.

And that's exactly what I did.

· · · · · · · · · · · · · · ·

I won the first tournament I entered as a professional.

A few days after I turned pro, my mother gave me the $300 entrance fee to the Missouri Open. Damned if I didn't go up there and win that sucker. My winner's check was for $6,700. I took it right home and tried to give it to Mom. She wouldn't take it. She wouldn't even take back the $300 she'd given me.

The next two months, I made about $28,000 in four events. I finished second in a playoff in a tournament in

Duncan, Oklahoma. Then in the top five at the Arkansas Open. A top 10 in the Oklahoma Open followed. Then another top five in St. Louis at a kind of Masters for the mini-tours.

I was practically on fire, right from the start, and the timing was perfect, because the next thing up was the PGA Tour Qualifying School, where I would earn my PGA Tour card for the 1988 season, which would let me start playing with the big boys.

Problem is, I flunked out.

Ask just about any professional golfer and he'll tell you that the toughest golf tournament he ever played in—by far—was Q-School.

Q-School is held every fall in three stages, for a total of 252 holes if you make it through the final stage. Last year, about 1,200 golfers competed for 30 PGA Tour cards for 2006. Get through Q-School and you get a shot at setting yourself up for life. This year, for example, if some new graduate of the 2005 Q-School finishes 125th on the 2006 money list, he'll make about $650,000—not counting sponsorship money and out-ings money—and he'll get a ticket to come back in 2007 and do it again.

And if you don't get through Q-School? Before 1990, when the PGA Tour set up its own developmental tour, you didn't have much choice but to hit the minitour circuit, where you'd hustle and scramble and grind your butt off for a year trying to cover expenses and trying to get your game ready for the next Q-School.

All that's at stake in Q-School is your future in golf.

I thought I was ready that first time, but Rick Ross, my sort of unofficial guru/teacher since I was a teenager, knew better. He'd tried to warn me how tough it was going to be, and to get me prepared if I didn't make it. You've got to be patient, John. You can't let a bad hole or a bad shot get you down, John. You've got to keep your focus, John.

Much as I loved and respected Rick—still do—all that shit just went in one ear and out the other.

Funny, though, I wasn't all that cut up. Surprised, shocked, disappointed—sure. But I didn't beat up on myself. I'd played good in the three months since I turned pro. I had a few bucks in my pocket. I figured I'd just keep on doing what I'd been doing the past three months, make a little money, and get my game ready for the next Q-School in the fall of 1988.

Hell, I was only 22. I still thought life was going to be easy.

So in 1988 I hit the minitour circuit. The way the minitours worked back then, you paid $1,200 to join an outfit called the PG Tour. (PG stood for Professional Golfers.) That entitled you to pony up $600 and play in any event run by any mini-tour that operated under the PG Tour umbrella. There were also all sorts of splinter tours and stand-alone pro events and state opens and things—all part of the big scramble.

Essentially what you were doing was playing for your own money, which was a guaranteed way to keep your attention. It was a helluva hard way to make a living. To cover expenses, you needed to make extra bucks in the money games you could always find at local clubs. But it was also a helluva good way to find out if you had the game and the guts to make it as a pro golfer.

There's nothing that focuses you more than playing to earn gas money for the trip to the next stop.

....

There'd been some great guys from South Africa on the golf team at Arkansas, and they told us how great it was playing over there on the Sunshine Tour, which ran from late December into early April. So when I missed the cut at Q-School again in 1988, I decided to go to South Africa and play the Sunshine Tour.

Problem was, it cost a bunch of money to get there, and then I'd need money to cover expenses until I won something, so I lined up a dozen people—my father-in-law and some friends of his—to kick in $1,000 apiece to keep me in water buffalo burgers, or whatever the hell they ate in South Africa that was the closest to Big Macs. The deal was that I would pay them back with interest from winnings.

It turned out to be a good deal for everybody concerned.

We played all over the country, which is almost twice the size of Texas. We played in Port Elizabeth, Durban, Johannesburg, and Cape Town, which is absolutely beautiful. That's where Peter Van Der Riet, my caddy, comes from. The ocean there could be the prettiest water I've ever seen in my life.

Nissan was one of the major sponsors of the Sunshine Tour, and they gave each player a car to drive through the country. That was great, but I was lucky I didn't kill myself because I wasn't used to driving on the wrong side of the road and I was drinking pretty heavy while I was there. Wrong side of the road and a lot of booze—not a good combo.

I finished in the top 10 in my first tournament in South Africa, which made me enough money to keep on playing the rest of the season. I kept on playing good, and by the time I was done, I'd made about $23,000 in eight events—enough to repay my backers, with a little stash left over. Plus, I finished 11th on the Sunshine Tour's Order of Merit, high enough so that I would be fully exempt in all their tournaments the following year if I wanted to come back.

I didn't figure I'd have to come back, because I planned on cruising through Q-School that fall, earning my card, and spending 1990 on the PGA Tour. But hey, you never know.

I had wanted my first wife, Dale, to go with me. We'd been married less than a year, and I wanted South Africa to be our big, exotic honeymoon. Only she wouldn't go. She'd gone with me to a few state opens and minitour events, but she hated the driving from one place to another, she hated walking around watching me play golf—who the hell did she think she'd married?—and she hated how much I was drinking. Plus, she hated the idea of being all the way across the world from her parents and friends. So she had stayed home.

Would I have had a better time if she'd gone? I don't know. Ordinarily, I really want my family to be with me when I'm on the road playing golf. That's one of the reasons I have my bus now. After I play and go through all the stuff associated with a tournament, like meeting with my sponsors and going to receptions and stuff like that, I like to go off to someplace where I feel at home, with my family around me. If I was by myself, I was a helluva lot more likely to spend the time partying and getting myself into trouble. Today, when I'm alone, I'm a lot more likely to go looking for a casino. (Thank God, gambling's not legal everywhere we play.)

But with me and Dale, I think we both figured out pretty quick that getting married was a mistake. I'm not sure I felt exactly relieved that she didn't go with me to South Africa, but I know I didn't miss her as much as I thought I would. And I'm pretty damned sure she didn't miss me. We separated soon after I returned home.

That first South African trip gave me just the dose of confidence I needed, not to mention a little financial cushion. In

1989 I made the cut at the U.S. Open in Rochester. Later that summer, I got into the Federal Express–St. Jude Classic in Memphis and the Chattanooga Classic on sponsors' exemptions, made the cut both places, and cashed checks for about $11,000 combined. I was feeling pretty damned good about my prospects again.

Right after Chattanooga, I got up at three in the morning to drive to Texarkana to play in a Monday event called the Insurance Youth Golf Classic. It was a one-day, four-ball event, with 20 pros, all young and green like me, and 60 junior golfers from all over the country. They paired us up in foursomes, one pro and three juniors. In my group there was this scrawny 13-year-old kid with a funny first name: Eldrick.

Yeah, that Eldrick.

The kid kicked my ass on the front nine, making the turn at three under while I shot one over. Wait a minute, who's the goddamned pro here, anyway? So I bore down on the back nine and he stumbled a little. I made four birdies, he made three bogeys, and I beat him by two strokes.

After it was over, I told the handful of local reporters covering the event that "this kid is great. I had heard a lot of good things about him but he's better than I'd heard." Tiger was still pissed about those three bogeys, I think, because he gave the pro in his foursome a little shot: "He didn't play a very smart game. He'd take a driver and go over trees and he'd hit hard sand wedges to par 5 greens."

(Yep, that was me back then. Now, too, for that matter.)

In 1990, when I went over to play the Sunshine Tour—yes, I missed the Q-School cut again—I took along one of my best buddies, Blake Allison, to caddy for me. We had us a helluva good time. We were out drinking and gambling and hell-raising just about every night. I mean, we were both in our early 20s, in a foreign country, seeing new places and people, and everything was an adventure.

I did some crazy things, some silly things. Once, a bunch of us were having dinner in this place with a giant buffet. Ronnie McCann, who I met there in South Africa and who's since become one of my best friends, happened to mention that it was his girlfriend's birthday. Hey, let's celebrate! I went over to the buffet line, and I picked up this big-ass chocolate cake and brought it back over to our table. Everybody started singing "Happy Birthday," but we didn't have any candles, so I poured a full glass of bourbon over the cake and just buried my face in it. I can't tell you why I did that—except maybe that I've always liked chocolate, especially Mom's chocolate gravy. And because it seemed like the right thing to do at the time. Whatever, people all around just laughed their ass off.

One night I'd been drinking really hard—and back then, that could have been just about any night—and I was pissed off about something. Me and Jimmy McGovern and a couple of other guys were going home late from some bar. He was riding shotgun, and I ran this red light, and then another one, and pretty soon I'm like, fuck it, and I just kept on going. The guys said later I ran through 17 straight reds before they could get me to pull over so somebody else could drive.

Later, I told that story to Rick Reilly of Sports Illustrated, and he said I set a new record for failed suicide attempts. Funny line. But if I did set the record, it's one I'm sure not proud of.

Anyway, I played even better this time and made some good money. And with that Nissan they let me use, me and Blake spent a lot of time just driving around. Hey, we were a couple of Arkansas bumpkins, not much more than kids, and South Africa felt like some big old playground to us.

One of the best times was when we went to this giant game park. It's like a million square miles of nothing but protected wild game. And we were driving along, real slow, and we came on this pack of orangutans. They looked a little scrawny, so Blake rolls down his window and throws a big handful of popcorn out. Next thing you know there are about a dozen of them all around the car and on the hood, pressing their faces up against the windows, flashing their big old fangs and gibbering and jabbering. And they just kept coming out of the bushes. In less than a minute, we had 20 or 30 of these hairy bastards—shit, it seemed like 200—crawling all over the car trying to get inside and get at that popcorn.

It would have been funny as hell if we hadn't been scared shitless. They weren't gorillas or anything, but they weren't cute little monkeys either. And up close, slobbering all over the windows and banging on the car, they looked huge. Finally, I just started driving away, real slow, and they started jumping off.

The lesson me and Blake learned right there was that when the sign as you enter a game park says "Do Not Feed the Animals," it means Do . . . NOT . . . Feed . . . the . . . Fucking Animals.

We saw a big herd of elephants. We saw hippos. We saw water buffaloes. We saw zebras and antelopes and giraffes.

We were like, this is like something out of a dream. It was like being in the middle of some big-ass zoo, only without cages or bars.

Then we came across a herd of lions. Actually, it's called a "pride" of lions, and now I understand why. We parked and watched them for almost three hours. There were probably 10 to 12 of them. One was just absolutely humongous. His mane was huge, and he had this big tuft of hair on his tail. This guy was definitely the boss of this outfit. So big, so beautiful. You got to remember, I'd never seen a lion before except in movies and picture books. I was just blown away.

It made me proud that my high school nickname was The Lion.

Me and Blake also saved a guy's life while we were in South Africa. Or at least we saved him from getting beat within an inch of his life. He was a caddy named Jumbo, who we'd gotten to know a little bit in tournaments. He had a regular bag, but the guy dropped off the tour with an injury, and Jumbo decided to go to the next stop—Pretoria, I think it was—and try to hook up with somebody.

Now, among caddies on the Sunshine Tour back then, that was a big no-no. It was okay to come to a tournament with the guy you were carrying for. It was not okay to come into town solo because if you did manage to get a bag, it would take away a job from one of the local guys who otherwise might have picked up that bag. The usual punishment for trying to poach like that, we discovered later, was for the caddies without bags to get together and beat the shit out of the poacher. You can sort of understand why: a professional tournament was the only chance local guys had all year to make a big paycheck.

Anyway, two days before the tournament was scheduled to begin, me and Blake had just pulled into the parking lot, which was near the first tee, and we were getting our gear out of the trunk when we spotted Jumbo running down the first fairway. Now, Jumbo came by his name honestly, but he was running like a fucking sprinter, no doubt because five or six other caddies with clubs in their hands were chasing his fat butt.

"Let's go!" I said to Blake. He dropped my clubs and we ran

back to the parking lot, hopped in the Nissan, and headed off down the fairway in what state troopers back home would call "high-speed pursuit." Guys were playing practice rounds, mind you, and this was an automobile, not a golf cart, steaming down the fairway. We passed the pack when they were about 10 yards behind Jumbo, and as we pulled alongside him, Blake opened the back door and hollered, "Jump in!"

We were fucking heroes, at least in our own minds—and Jumbo's.

The golf my second season on the Sunshine Tour was pretty sweet, too. People remembered me from the year before and cheered me. I had a couple of top 10s. And I won a tournament in Johannesburg and got a big check: $16,000. Me and Blake then went up to Swaziland. When we arrived, I got word that my divorce from Dale was final. Although we'd split up a year earlier, I guess hearing it was final hit me pretty hard. Or maybe I was just relieved. I don't know.

Either way, I shot 66 in the first round, but then went to the casino and pissed away most of my money—something like $25,000. In other words, what I'd just won at Johannesburg plus a big chunk of what I'd made the whole month before. I was pissed, royally pissed. Wouldn't you be? And drunk as hell, too. And probably, deep down inside, hurting because my marriage had gone belly-up.

So I went back up to my hotel room and beat the shit out of it. Trashed it pretty good, the kind of thing I've done too many times in my life when I've lost control. This time, though, I put my fist through a TV set and damned near ended my career before it got started.

They took me to the hospital, where a doctor patched me up. I'd cracked a bone or two, and cut myself up pretty bad. The doctor who worked on me said that with a thing like that, a combination of impact and the glass, I could have destroyed some tendons and shit and pretty much fucked up my hand forever. He told me I was lucky. And he also told me to withdraw from the tournament. He said I shouldn't touch a golf club until my hand healed.

Fuck that. I was at the top of the leaderboard, I'd been playing great golf, and I sure as hell needed the money after blowing my bankroll at the casino the night before. Blake had to leave me in the hospital to go back to the hotel to deal with the shit storm I'd unleashed, and I told him as he left, don't worry, son—I'm going to go out there and win this sonofabitch.

And I did.

(Funny thing, I had to do it without Blake on my bag. He got spooked about having to deal with the hotel people and maybe cops in a foreign country, so he went straight from the hospital back to Johannesburg. I had to scrounge up a caddy at the golf course. Don't think I didn't give Blake some serious shit for being such a wuss when we hooked up back in Johannesburg.)

Another $16,000 winner's check brought me back almost to where I started the weekend, and I had enough to cover the $1,000 or so the hotel charged me for busting the TV and wrecking the room. All in all, not a bad topper for my second swing on the Sunshine Tour.

South Africa took some of the pressure off of trying to survive those two years. I had some good times there, made some good money, saw another part of the world, met some people who are still good friends—and I didn't die of alcohol poisoning that time in Swaziland, didn't get myself thrown out of the country for busting up that hotel room, didn't wreck my hand permanently, and didn't get eaten up by those big apes.

All in all, a great success.

....

That spring, just after I got back from South Africa, I headed out to play the new Hogan Tour that the PGA Tour had launched in 1990 as its own, official version of a minitour—or, as they preferred to call it, a "developmental tour." I had qualified for it by finishing high enough up in the 1989 Q-School.

The Hogan Tour had bigger purses, stronger fields, and a longer schedule than any of the minis. They sold it as one of those "stars of tomorrow" things and as a "stepping-stone" to the PGA Tour, and in some of the smaller towns it went into, the Hogan Tour actually drew some galleries. That was nice: on your average minitour stop, the only people watching you play would be wives and girlfriends.

The Hogan later became the Nike Tour for a while; today it's called the Nationwide Tour. And it's one of the best things the PGA Tour ever did for improving the quality of the game.

I thought I'd take the Hogan Tour by storm. I know that sounds arrogant, but I was coming off a strong season in South Africa, where I'd won twice, and I just thought, okay, it's finally coming together, I'm finally going to play my way onto the PGA Tour. Only early on, it didn't go exactly the way I'd figured. I played some decent golf, and some not so decent. I'd struggled with my game from time to time before, but this time I hadn't expected to have to struggle, and I got down on myself pretty bad.

So one day in the early part of the summer, between tournaments, I dropped by the Bay Ridge Golf Club in Dardanelle to talk to Dandy Cline. (He'd been Mr. Don Cline when I was a teenager, but now that I was "all grown up"—never mind that I didn't always act like it—I called him Dandy, after Dandy Don Meredith.) He'd always been there for me and my brother. He was as much a father to me as my own father was when I was a teenager, and I knew I could level with him.

I told Dandy I was thinking of not finishing out the summer on the Hogan Tour. There was some long hauls coming up, first to Amarillo way out in West Texas, then north and west all the way up to Utah. I told Dandy I was unhappy with my game, that maybe I wasn't as good as I thought I was, and that maybe I should start looking around for a club job and settle down. I'd been divorced from Dale for a while by then, and I was just flat-out lonely. I was drinking pretty hard, of course—I didn't tell Dandy that, but I didn't have to. And I was just generally feeling like a worthless piece of shit.

Looking back, I must have sounded like some sorry, whiny, pitiful, mully-grubbing sonofabitch, and I guess I was. I mean, I'd been through worse stretches before, (and God knows, I would go through worse stretches after), and I hadn't gone crying on anybody's shoulder. It wasn't my style. My style was just to get drunk and beat the shit out of something.

Anyway, I tell Dandy all this, and he just sits there, taking it all in. He doesn't say anything at first, and then finally he looks me in the eye and he says, "John, there's nothing else in the world you'd rather do with your life than play golf, am I right?" (I nod.) "Then get your butt back out there and play golf. You're a professional golfer, John. Go play golf."

I don't know what I'd expected Dandy to say, but I do know that what he did say was exactly the right thing. I got my butt back out there. I played good in Amarillo, not so good a couple of other places. And then I drove all the way up to Utah and won the damned tournament and a check for $20,000, my biggest payday since I turned pro in 1987.

Thank you, Dandy. You've heard me say those words before,

but I can never say them enough for what you've done for me over the years.

For me, 1990 was what you might call a pivotal year. I won twice on the Sunshine Tour in South Africa. I got divorced. I wrecked my first hotel room. I met the woman who would become the second Mrs. John Daly. (You'll meet her in Chapter 7.) I managed to survive another trip to an ER to be treated for alcohol poisoning (this time in Falmouth, Maine). I almost quit golf. I won a Hogan Tour tournament. I finished high enough on the Hogan Tour money list to earn to the final stage of the 1990 Q-School.

Oh, and did I mention that I made the cut at Q-School and earned my PGA Tour card for 1991?

Yes! Finally!

Q-School, as far as I'm concerned, ought to be considered the fifth major. So many good golfers, so much pressure, so much riding on the outcome. And it's not just a bunch of wide-eyed kids chasing a dream, like I was in 1990 (and 1989 and 1988 and 1987). Last year, Larry Mize had to go to Q-School. Yeah, *that* Larry Mize, the 1987 Masters champion. He didn't make the final cut, so in 2006 his status on the PGA Tour will be Past Champion, which is at the bottom of the barrel in terms of getting into events. He'll also get some sponsors' exemptions, because he's a great guy and a former Masters champion. But a lot of other really good golfers, guys who've been on the Tour before but lost their cards, didn't make the cut either, and they'll spend the year scrambling hard.

Hell, if I don't have a good year in 2006, I could be back in Q-School next fall.

And I've already told you how much I hated school.

•••••••••••••••

My first PGA Tour event as an official, bona fide, card-carrying member of the PGA Tour was the Northern Telecom Open in Tucson in the second week of January 1991. By then I'd played in a handful of Tour events, of course, and I'd even won some money. But this was the first time I felt like I belonged, not like I was some side order of vegetables that nobody ordered. Problem is, I played like shit: 73, 79—cut.

Oh, the guy who won that tournament? Some gangly college kid from Arizona State, the last amateur to win an official PGA Tour event. You've probably heard of him: a lefty swinger from California named Phil Mickelson.

The first cut I made as a member of the PGA Tour—shit, I still remember how it felt saying those last five words back then—came at my second tournament, two weeks later, at the United Hawaiian Open. I shot 66, 72, 72 in the first three rounds and was all set to go low on Sunday and crack the top 20, but then I went out and shot myself in the foot with a 77. Still, while T-69 wasn't anything to write home about, it was the first cut I made as a *member of the PGA Tour.*

The next four tournaments were up and down—two missed cuts, a T-60, and a T-20 (at Pebble Beach, of all places, where I've since had a pretty ugly history). Then it was all the way back across the country to Florida and the Honda Classic.

Honda was my breakout tournament. After Honda, I knew I belonged out there, and all of a sudden so did a lot of other people. I shot 68, 68, 76, 71 to finish at T-4. Man, except for that 76, I would have been this close to my first PGA Tour win.

The only downside is that a win there in Florida would have taken a lot of the surprise out of what took place the following August up in Indiana.

○ ○ ○ ○ ○ ○

FOUR

A LONG, LONG WAY . . .

There's an old country song that goes "It's a long, long way to the top of the world/But it's only a short fall back down." Well, in the three years after I won the 1991 PGA, I found out how short that fall was. And how painful.

At first, everything was great. The cash poured in like a cow pissing on a flat rock. All of a sudden, I was being offered tons of money to show up for Monday and Tuesday corporate outings and fund-raisers. I was getting paid $25,000, $50,000, $75,000 a pop to hang with golf lovers for half a day. Shit, I was in hog heaven.

To put it in perspective, the first-ever corporate outing I did was earlier that year after I finished T-4 at Honda. I guess word had gotten around about this big redneck rookie who could hit the ball a long ways, and some outfit up in Syracuse, New York, asked me to come up to their event. I was paid $1,500.

Funny what winning a major can do for a pro golfer's market value.

Best of all was getting into all the big-money events at the end of the year. They call it the Silly Season, but they ought to call it the Money Season. It starts, really, with the Tour

Championship, the last official PGA Tour tournament of the year. The field is limited to the top 30 finishers on the money list. In 2005, last place in the Tour Championship paid $105,300. Finish first in 2006 and you'll haul away $1,170,000. In 1991, I finished third and picked up a cool $138,000.

But I was only just getting warmed up. I went to Australia for a big appearance fee. Then I came home and won $128,000 and two new cars in the Skins Game playing with Jack Nicklaus, Curtis Strange, and Payne Stewart. I played in Japan at the Dunlop Phoenix, which is a big tournament over there. Then, in December, I went off to South Africa for the Million Dollar Golf Challenge in Sun City. (Got a big appearance fee, finished eighth, lost about $150,000 at the casino, got hammered, trashed my hotel room.) And then there were the corporate outings: Monday here, Tuesday there—more big checks, like found money.

Overnight, I was the hottest property in golf.

Best of all were the sponsorship deals. I had signed with Ping when I came on the tour in 1991. Ping had a point system—you didn't get guaranteed money, but you got points for how well you played using the company's gear. For example, I made $230,000 for winning with the PGA—and that was great money, don't get me wrong—but I made another $236,000 in 1991 just for playing with Ping clubs and wearing a Ping shirt and a Ping hat. And that was only the beginning.

Early in 1992, I signed my first really big sponsorship contract, a 10-year deal with Wilson that paid me millions of dollars a year. There were bonuses for wins, top 10 finishes, cuts made, appearances, and other stuff. At the time it was made, it was probably the biggest golf equipment sponsorship deal ever. Not bad for a guy who, 18 months earlier, had been hacking away on the Hogan Tour, trying to cover expenses.

Mainly, in the 18 months or so after Crooked Stick, I was just enjoying life. All of the stuff I used to worry about, like finding the closest Motel 6 or Red Roof Inn to the tournament I was playing in that week, was history. All of a sudden it was, hey, Mr. Daly, if you stay at such and such swank hotel this week, we'll give you the room free. Shit like that blew my mind.

Another great thing about the PGA Tour—I don't know about the other guys, but I didn't realize this until I got out there in 1991—is you get a free courtesy car each week. And you get free food at the tournament. And you get all this free stuff in your locker—golf balls, gloves, shirts, gifts from the tournament sponsors, offers to give clinics, all sorts of goodies you couldn't imagine. The first time I ate in a clubhouse at a tournament, I asked for my check and the waiter said, "Oh, no, Mr. Daly. You're fine. No check." All you had to do was leave a tip.

As a rookie, getting free food was maybe the coolest thing. Shit, I'd been playing the minitours for two years and the Hogan for one and no matter where you went, you paid. Play golf and all you can eat free? I still get excited just thinking about it.

The money was coming from everywhere. My agents lined it up, and we went for it. We had to go for it. I mean, shit, it was like the golden egg. It just fell in my lap and I said, hell, I'm going to take advantage of all of it. Who knew if it would last? I'd always wanted to see other parts of the country and the world anyhow. Bring it on! Bring it *all* on!

Australia was my first big trip overseas as PGA Champion. It's a beautiful, beautiful country. I loved the people. But the golf courses there bit me in the ass—hard. The first tournament I played Down Under was the Australian Masters, and back then all I knew how to do was just hit driver. But if you miss the fairway on most Australian courses, you're dead meat. You're in the bush, all sticky thorns and shit. Hit in there and you might as well just re-tee. Even if you find your ball, you won't be able take an unplayable because you won't be able to find a place to drop.

So that first time at the Australian Masters, I shot 81 in the second round and was disqualified for not signing my scorecard. I hit driver on every hole except the par 3s because I didn't know any better—that's just the way I had taught myself to play. No way I was going to make the cut, but I felt bad about the DQ because these people had paid me a lot of money to come down there and play. I was embarrassed. I got fined by the PGA Tour for the DQ: my first fine, but—Lord help me—not my last.

Pretty much since the PGA win, fans everywhere wanted one thing: to see me hit driver. I'd step up to a tee and they'd all be yelling, "Kill it, John! Grip it and rip it!" Like a big idiot, I listened to them and pulled out my driver even when I knew better—and ended up making a lot of big numbers all through 1992. I did shoot 18 under to win the B.C. Open that year, which was a big relief because, okay, now the monkey's off my back, I'm not just a one-win wonder.

The first four majors I entered as the winner of a major myself were something special. Not for the golf I played, which mostly sucked, but because I got to hear my name being announced on the first tee: "John Daly, 1991 PGA Champion." I couldn't get enough of that.

The thing that surprised me most about Augusta National, seeing it the first time, was how hilly it is. If you've only seen it on TV, you don't have any idea how up and down the place is. And you used not to get to see the front nine on TV at all.

I finished T-19 in my first Masters at five under, with a 68 on the final round. I was pretty happy about that. I felt like I could have scored better, but that 68 on Sunday got me feeling that Augusta was a course I was going to master someday. A lot of other people thought so, too. I still love it, even if it hasn't quite worked out that way—yet.

The U.S. Open in 1992 was my second as a pro, my third overall. My first Open, back when I was a sophomore at Arkansas, I didn't come close to making the cut at Shinnecock Hills. The second time, at Oak Hill in Rochester, I made the cut but finished in the back of the pack, at T-69. This time, at Pebble Beach, I went 74-75—cut.

The British Open that year was at Muirfield, one tough-ass golf course. Tough but fair. I drained a 20-foot par putt on the 18th hole of the second round to make the cut right on the nose. Then it was 80-75 on the weekend, and . . . what time does our plane leave?

Naturally, I wanted to play good at the PGA as the defending champion. This year it was at Bellerive Country Club in St. Louis. Instead, 76-72-79-77. From 1st to 82nd. I wasn't too happy. But hey, it is what it is.

Basically, my golf game in 1992 played second fiddle to making money—at outings, from appearance fees, from sponsorships—and partying. Instead of partying, I guess I ought to just say drinking, which is what it was. For the first time in my life, I let my golf game slide. That whole year, I don't think I practiced more than two days in a row. And it showed. Sure, I won the B.C. Open in late September, but I missed 10 cuts in 25 tournaments.

You can't do much on the PGA Tour if you spend too many Saturday mornings watching cartoons.

....

Like I said, I was drinking a lot. It wasn't like in college or in South Africa or on the minitours. It wasn't a fifth a day, not close. In 1992, if I was playing decent, it was like, hey, I've got to be sharp tomorrow. But if I missed a cut or had a blow-up round on Saturday or Sunday, it was like, hey, let's see how fast I can get shit-faced. I drank mostly when I was mad at myself for the way I was playing.

And in 1992 and 1993, that was most of the time.

Some people said and wrote at the time that John Daly, he must be depressed. Well, I don't remember feeling sad all the time, even when things got rough. That's being depressed, right? Being sad all the time? I laughed a lot. Still do. I got along with people. Still do. I don't remember sitting around thinking about my troubles. Angry? You bet your ass. I'm angry a lot. Sometimes I feel like I'm gonna bust, I get so pissed off. Times like that, I sometimes take it out on walls and TV sets and cars.

But I don't see that as being depressed or sad.

I see it as being mad.

Despite all the money that was pouring in and my win at the B.C. Open, what made 1992 such a downer was that horseshit, blown-out-of-proportion thing in Colorado when, right before Christmas, I destroyed my house and got accused (and convicted, at least in the press) of domestic abuse.

My guess is you probably heard about it or read about it, maybe back then, or more likely in some of the million news-papers and magazines that have dredged it up in just about every article or feature story written about me since. But I guaran-damn-tee you've never heard the entire, completely true story, because I've never had a real chance to tell it before now. Actually, I have told it before, to a bunch of sportswriters, but it's always come out in bits and pieces, all twisted and screwed up.

So here's what really happened. It's not pretty, and I'm not proud of it, but it is what it is, and not what they said it was at the time.

Let me tee it up for you.

In August 1992, after the International in Castle Pines, Colorado, I bought a new house right next to the golf course. It was an impulse buy, no doubt about it. I didn't exactly think it through—I mean, living in a place where you can't practice for four or five months a year is maybe not the most brilliant choice of residence a professional golfer could make. But I'd finished fifth in the tournament, and I was feeling pretty good after a bad stretch when I missed four straight cuts before stinking up the British and the PGA. Plus, I had all this money now, and I was hoping that me and Bettye and Shynah could make a fresh start in a new place. Me and Bettye had been having serious, serious troubles—I'll get into all that shit in Chapter 7—and I told her, Baby, let's just start over and try and make it work.

Castle Pines is a drop-dead beautiful golf course in a beautiful part of a beautiful state. And the people who own it, the Vickers family, are really beautiful people. Plus, I'd fallen in love the fall before with the Broncos and Denver coach Dan Reeves, the former Cowboy. Steve Atwater, who had played for Arkansas, was a defensive back for the Broncos. We were good buddies. The week of the tournament, I got to throw the ball around with John Elway a little bit. I went out to a Broncos practice and they let me kick field goals; Coach

Reeves said if I made three straight 35-yarders, he'd cut practice short. I did, and the guys practically carried me off the field.

New home, new part of the country, new football team to follow, new place to try to make my marriage work—that's the way I saw Castle Pines. I even took a pass on some of the Silly Season events because I wanted to stay with Bettye and the baby in Castle Pines and try to patch things up.

In four months, it all turned to shit.

Fact is, and I should have realized this—things between me and Bettye were going downhill too fast for anything to turn it around. We fought all that fall, about anything and everything. I'd pretty much had my fill of it, and I went back to Dardanelle to get away from her. Then Bettye called and said I should come on back so we could at least spend Shynah's first Christmas together as a family. I said okay, fine, and me and Jamie and his girlfriend hauled ass back to Castle Pines.

Big mistake.

Well, we decided to have a Christmas party on December 19. We had a bunch of people over: Sean Pacetti, a guy I knew from the Hogan Tour; my old grade-school buddy, Donnie Crabtree, and his girlfriend; Dan Hampton, the great Chicago Bears defensive end and good friend of mine, and his fiancée, Julie—maybe a dozen people in all. It's what you do before Christmas, right? You have a big party.

Everybody's having a good time—drinking, eating, dancing, listening to music, shooting pool, partying away. We're all down in the rec room, and I'm dancing and sort of bumping with Julie a little bit, and Dan's bumping with me, and we're all just having a good time, when all of a sudden Bettye comes down and yells out, "Why don't you just go fuck her?" And I go, "What are you talking about? Watch your mouth! She's

Dan's fiancée!" But Bettye, she just keeps on yelling and cursing me and screaming at Julie that it's her fucking house and she better not forget it, making everybody miserable. Dan and Julie go upstairs to get away from her, and then Bettye goes back up to her room.

And I just lost it.

What I did was, I destroyed my house. I punched through the poolroom walls. I kicked in a 57-inch TV set. I smashed up my trophy case. I wrecked my office. I ripped off the cupboard doors in the kitchen and threw all the pots and pans on the floor and smashed all the dishes and glasses. I just took the whole place apart.

Now, Bettye had been upstairs the whole time I was doing this. Then she comes back down and yells at me to stop, and I yell at her to go fuck herself, and I walk past her and bump up against her, and I keep on demolishing the place. But I didn't hit her. I did *not* hit her.

Finally, I turned to my brother Jamie and said let's get out of this place, and we piled into my car and headed back to Arkansas.

By now, somebody had called 911, and the cops came, and the place was in shambles. They reported it as a "scene of domestic violence." Bettye said she didn't want to press charges or anything, but she did say I pushed her against a wall and pulled her hair, which was absolute bullshit. But the cops believed her and they were looking to arrest me for battery and harassment. And I've got to haul my ass back from Arkansas or they're going to put out an arrest warrant on me.

How crazy is that? Bettye didn't want to press any charges. She told the cops I never hit her. Everybody else at the party said I never hit her. She'd even called me before the cops made their move to tell me she wanted me to come back for

Christmas. And all of a sudden, I'm a criminal, and I better turn myself in or they're going to drag me away in chains?

The media, of course, immediately branded me as a wife abuser, even though Bettye issued a formal statement through her lawyer to the prosecuting attorney trying to get the charges against me dropped: "I was not struck or physically injured in the incident. I neither reported the incident nor requested the sheriff's department to intervene." But the prosecutor said that in his jurisdiction they weren't in a habit of dropping domestic violence charges, even when the alleged victim refused to cooperate—and even though, from what I can tell, there was no evidence that she was a "victim" of anything in the first place.

So what I finally did in the spring, just to make the whole thing go away, I pled guilty to harassment and was sentenced to two years of probation.

Guilty? Bullshit.

Convict me for disturbing the peace—fine. Convict me for wrecking my own house—fine. But anything having anything to do with domestic abuse? Fuck that. For the next month or so, of course, everything you heard about me was that I was some kind of monster. "John Daly" and "domestic abuse"— those four words seemed to be locked together.

And you know, that shit went on and on. Years later, I was in the Horseshoe Casino down in Tunica, Mississippi, on the Gulf Coast, and as a friend and I were walking past some people, I heard some woman say, "Yeah, that's him. That's the wife abuser, the golfer." My friend stopped and said, "You know what, lady? You just don't know your facts."

And just last year some jerk sportswriter in Florida hauled out the Colorado thing. He wrote that I'd been accused of "domestic violence" back in 1992. I was not accused of "domestic violence." The guy can't even pick up a phone and check out his damned facts? I'm suing him and the paper that printed his lies.

That shit hurts, man. I never hit Bettye. I never hit any woman. I never will. There's lots of things I won't say I'll never do because, you know, I just might. But I will never hit a woman. Period.

Over the years, I've caught plenty of hell for bad shit I've actually done. That's fine. That's the way it should be. If I do something, I'm willing to take responsibility. But you'd think there was enough bad stuff that I *have* done to write about without working me over for shit I didn't do.

What it comes down to is this, which is what I told a guy from *Sports Illustrated*: You remember that time when Richard Pryor said he killed his car?

Well, that's what I did in Colorado: I killed my house.

But I did not hit, hurt, or in any physical way abuse my wife.

. . . .

Nothing I said about my side of this thing cut any ice with Deane Beman, the commissioner of the PGA Tour.

A few days after the Colorado shit hit the fan, he called me up and laid out my options: agree to leave the tour "voluntarily" and get "professional help" or be fined and suspended indefinitely.

What choice did I really have? On December 29, 1992, I issued a statement through the PGA Tour:

I deeply regret the incident at my home over the holidays. I realize the importance of seeking professional help and therefore I will pursue counseling immediately for an alcohol-related problem. I will check into an alcohol rehabilitation facility and will return to tournament play only when I am comfortable my life is in order.

(You think that sounds like me? Just asking.)

The next day, I got in my car and started driving from Denver to Arizona to this rehab center called Sierra Tucson. I was going "voluntarily," but I sure as hell didn't want to go.

A few miles outside of Castle Pines, I called Donnie Crabtree on the car phone. I told him I was sick to death of the whole shooting match. There was a big cliff up ahead, and I pulled over facing the edge. I told Donnie that my life was shit and I might as well gun the damned car over the guardrail. Donnie said, "You didn't do anything but beat the shit out of your own house. You didn't touch Bettye. Don't even think about what you're thinking about doing."

I don't know whether I was *really* thinking about driving over the cliff and killing myself. Maybe—no, probably—I just wanted to hear somebody I loved and who cared about me tell me I wasn't a worthless piece of shit and that I should get myself together and deal with it. We must have talked for half an hour, me and Donnie, before I headed on to Tucson.

I checked into Sierra Tucson in early January 1993 and stayed there for three weeks. As I said, I did it "voluntarily." I learned some things. I met a very strong individual, Thomas "Hollywood" Henderson, the former Dallas Cowboys star, who became a very important person in my life. And later, I named my second daughter Sierra.

But you know what? I went there for the wrong reasons. I went because other people told me to. I went to get Deane Beman off my back. He would have suspended me if I hadn't gone in on my own. I do know that my conclusion after those 18 days was, hell, I'm not the one who's fucked up here.

The truth is, I should never have said I was an alcoholic.

That's right: I believe now that I should never have admitted I was an alcoholic. I only did it because that's what you're supposed to do in rehab. I did it to appease people, not because I thought I really was one. I don't know for sure what I thought, to tell the truth, or what actually was going through my mind. I mean, you're sitting around in these group sessions with these screwed-up people telling their sad stories, and it gets to the point where it's, you know, okay, just to not look like an idiot, I'm going to say I'm an alcoholic.

Meanwhile, all the time I was there, me and Bettye were sneaking off together. Since the day we'd met back in 1990, we'd always been superactive sexually, but for something like three weeks after Colorado, we'd been sort of estranged. She was staying in one of these villas on the property that Sierra Tucson has for spouses and family, but you're not supposed to see each other or get together or anything while one party is in rehab. Only me and Bettye, we were being ourselves, so I snuck out of my window at night and went over to her place and we got it on pretty good.

We even got back together for a while after I left Sierra Tucson, but we didn't stay together long. Bettye filed divorce papers that spring and I was, fine, let's get it done. I was glad to be shut of all the mistrust and the lies, but I'll say this: despite all the shit that went down, sex was never a problem between us.

The thing is, I had to go to rehab so fast that there was no way I could really defend myself to the media and everybody on that deal. I should have given myself time to at least been able to tell my side of what happened. I'm not going to sit here and lie to you and say that I didn't destroy my house. I *did* destroy my house. But I didn't put anybody in harm's way. I mean, Dan Hampton's a pretty strong boy. He could take care of himself and a mess of other folks at the same time. But he didn't have to. I was mad out of my mind, but all I attacked was my house, not people. Dan did finally manage to get me calmed down. But by then, though, somebody had called the police.

On the way back to Arkansas after me and my brother decided to get the hell away from Colorado, Jamie said to me, "This is bullshit, John. You oughtn't to live here; you need to live where it's warm. You don't need the fucking snow." Jamie was right, of course. Always as a kid I got crazy when it got cold. I always wanted to go somewhere where I could play golf all the time. So what the hell was I doing living in Colorado? All I can say is I made some pretty dumb decisions back in those years, and Colorado was one of them.

Unfortunately, it wouldn't be the last.

. . . .

Every year, usually the Monday and Tuesday after the International, Peter Jacobsen used to host this great charity event in Portland called the Fred Meyer Challenge. It always attracted a great field because Peter's such a great host. He threw this great party every year where he and his band, Jake Trout and the Flounders, would entertain about a thousand people in this humongous tent with some good old rock-and-roll. Peter was the lead singer and played guitar. Payne Stewart used to be one of the Flounders.

But even more fun was the "golf clinic" Jake put on for the fans before the tournament. People jammed temporary grandstands behind the first tee, and Jake stood on the tee box and did this funny-ass routine where he mimicked the swings of a lot of the guys. He used to do a terrific Arnold Palmer, where he would take this vicious hack, then bring the club back and turn his head way over to the side. (Close your eyes, think of Arnie hitting driver. See?) And he did a killer Craig Stadler, with a towel stuffed up under his sweater. Then, with everybody in a good mood, he'd bring out a few pros to demonstrate different kinds of shots—you know, a cut, a draw, a banana slice, a straight-up L-wedge, that sort of shit. It gave the crowd a good demonstration, and it gave us a chance to show off.

Well, it was after this part of the show that I did something that got me up to my ass in hot water.

As you'd figure, Peter asked me to come out and demonstrate hitting driver. He set me up real good, cracking jokes about this and that, and I played along because I wanted to put on a good show for the fans. Only when I went to hit my drive, I turned around and set up facing the fans in the stands. I made a big production of it, taking my time, loosening up my shoulders, and waggling my Killer Whale (the Wilson driver I used at the time). The fans were cheering and whooping and eating it up. Kill it, Big John! Grip it and rip it! One guy in the back row, he stood up and held his arms up like he was a goalpost. And so I stood up to the ball and let 'er rip.

I think everybody thought it was going to be one of those fake exploding balls. It wasn't. It was one of my John Daly Wilson Staff signature babies, and I caught it good. It cleared the stands by a good 50 feet—splitting the uprights—and ended up in the parking lot about 300 yards away.

People went nuts. They loved it.

Deane Beman went nuts, too. Only he hated it.

John, that'll cost you $30,000.

Looking back, I can see that maybe it was not the smartest thing to do. But honest to God, I hadn't coldcocked a line drive off the tee since I was 15 years old. There wasn't a chance in hell I was going to hurt anybody. I was just trying to show them a good time. But I surprised the shit out of Peter, and I shocked a few other people as well.

P.S.: The next year, we did use one of those fake exploding golf balls. People didn't like it half as much.

What I did in November 1993 at the Lincoln-Mercury Kapalua Invitational, though, was just plain stupid. I picked up my golf ball on the 11th green without putting out and walked to the 12th tee. I knew better. I was pissed off. I'd four-putted three times already—*four-putted!* The tournament was set up as a pro-am, and in the pro-ams we play every week, you pick up your ball when the hole is settled, and . . . shit, I feel like an idiot trying to explain it now, because it was a bone-head move then and it's still a bonehead move now, 13 years later. I knew I had to keep score. I knew it wasn't a regular Wednesday pro-am. But I picked up my ball and went to the next tee and hit my tee shot before somebody came up to me and said, "John, what the hell are you doing?"

I apologized and all, but Deane wasn't hearing any of it: he fined me $30,000 and slapped me with an indefinite suspension. Well, I'd done plenty of things that were worse and never got punished so hard, but I know Beman didn't like me, so he took his best shot. Last place was like, $7,650, so I go, "Just give that to charity as well."

Fact is, that suspension might have been a good thing in disguise. Since winning the PGA in 1991, I never worked hard on my game for a good, solid week. I was too busy going here and there and everywhere, picking up big checks. I don't blame myself for that. My job as a professional is to make my living from golf, right? But I got to use the time off for working on my game, so the suspension may have been a blessing. In one stretch I worked eight straight days in Palm Springs, six and a half hours a day, practicing hard.

(Thank you, Deane.)

But what gave me a bad case of the red ass wasn't the size of the fine or even the suspension, but the idea it planted in people's heads that I was drinking again. In announcing the suspension, the PGA Tour office said I'd been "advised to seek counseling," some bullshit like that, and everybody took it to mean that I was drinking again. Uh-uh. I wasn't. I was nearly two years sober, and I was playing like shit, and I felt like shit because of the antidepressants I was taking, but I wasn't drinking.

I wanted to be drinking. I wanted to drink a lot. But I didn't.

All I can say about 1993 is that there was no 1993, at least not in terms of golf. The only good thing was that I had been sober a year. That had been my goal, and I achieved it. Golf? The best thing I did all year was reach the 630-yard 17th at Baltusrol in the U.S. Open in two—driver, 1-iron.

That was fucking historic. The rest of the year was shit.

• • • • • • • • • • • • • •

Guess what? The following year, 1994, after a good start, didn't finish any better than 1993.

My suspension was lifted in March. I returned to the Tour at the Honda Classic where, rusty as I was, I finished T-4. (Take that, Deane.) Then I scuffed it around—a T-21, two cuts, and a T-48 in my next four tournaments—before posting a T-7 in Houston and an honest-to-God, I-haven't-forgotten-how-after-all win at the BellSouth Classic in Atlanta. But the rest of the year slid down the crapper. In my last eight tournaments, I had four cuts, one WD, and one DQ.

It was another year of personal hell. I was on antidepressants that were fucking me up, giving me the shakes and the sweats and diarrhea. I was miserable. I was gambling—and I was eating chocolate like a madman.

There were times after I'd stopped drinking JD when I'd get a sugar craving so bad at night in my hotel room that I'd call down and have them open up the gift shop and send me all the M&M's they had. Man, I'd suck down anything chocolate: chocolate ice cream, chocolate shakes, chocolate cake, chocolate chip cookies, Butterfingers, you name it. Sometimes I'd eat 15, 20 packs of M&M's a round (with peanuts). When I won the British in 1995, I ate chocolate chip muffins and chocolate croissants all day long, every day of the tournament.

At rehab, they call it cross-addiction. They warn you that when you give up one thing, like whiskey, you're going to be looking to replace it with something else. They say you go from one addiction to another. For me, when I stopped drinking I started eating more chocolate and gambling more.

A lot more.

One made me fat. The other damned near bankrupted me.

The gambling started big-time after I came out of rehab in January 1993. My home in Memphis is about 45 minutes from the casinos in Tunica, Mississippi, on the Gulf Coast. There's a Tour stop in Vegas. There's a Tour stop in Reno. From anywhere on the West Coast swing, it's a quick bump over to Vegas or Reno. I know. Beginning in 1994, that's where I spent a lot of my spare time and even more of my money.

By the end of the year, I had won about $340,000 on the Tour but I managed to lose about $4 million—*four million dollars*—at the casinos.

The year was good because I stayed sober. On just about every other count, it sucked.

There's a saying that bad press is as good as good press, and some of the bad press may have helped me in a lot of ways. I mean, I get along with most of the guys who cover the Tour—most of the regular guys, who are around a lot—because I don't give them any shit. They ask me a question, I answer it. You want "No comment," go talk to some other guy.

But I get burned sometimes when some guy starts talking to me and it turns out he has an agenda. Or when somebody drags up something out of ancient history—that really pisses me off. I mean, how many times do I have to go over some of the bad shit I did 5, even 10 years ago?

C'mon guys, gimme a break. I know I've got some *new* bad shit you can write about, if you'd just do your homework. Actually, that's not true. The last five years, about the only bad shit you'd have to write about involves me and my putter.

Probably the worst hosing I ever got from the press came in Scotland, in 1994, and I have to admit that I was in part to blame. Here's what a reporter said I said. My agent still has the clip, probably as a caution to me not to blow off my big mouth so much:

> There are certain people on the Tour who do the crazy stuff. They're never going to get exposed unless they are found out by the police and put in jail.... I wish we could have drug testing on the Tour. If we did, I'd probably be one of the cleanest guys out there.... Drugs, cocaine, some of the other crazy things. If you're going to test everybody, athletes in the NBA, football players for steroids, test the golfers. Let it come out.... I think it's unfair that a lot of this stuff has been hidden. If we did

introduce tests, it would help the guys with the problems, not hurt them.

When I read that, I flipped out. I'm not saying I didn't say it, but I'm damned sure I didn't mean it the way it came out. I tried to clear it up the next day: "I don't know of anybody who uses drugs on the Tour, but I have heard rumors. I don't know it, but I believe it." But that didn't help.

You know what that was? That was me on Prozac. I was on that fucking drug at the time, and I was miserable, and I just fired off shit without thinking before I opened my big mouth. A lot of guys got pissed—and rightly so. Curtis Strange said, "John Daly should crawl back under the rock where he came from." Greg Norman was pissed, but he did the right thing— he got in my face and asked me, man to man, just what in the fuck I was talking about. I told him that all I meant to get across was that alcohol wasn't the only thing being abused out there, and that maybe the Tour should take a long look at itself. Greg—who had been ready to kick my ass, I think—was cool with that.

Curtis? We haven't been exactly best buds since.

Sometime near the end of the year, some golf writer wrote, "John Daly used to be contender. Now he's just a curiosity."

That hurt, but I couldn't argue with it.

What I could do was prove him wrong.

FIVE

○ ○ ○ ○ ○ ○

THE LION IN HIS DEN

The middle of the summer, it stays light real late in Scotland.
About 8:30, just before sunset on the Wednesday of British
Open Week in 1995, I was standing with my agent Bud
Martin outside the door of my room on the first floor of the
Old Course Hotel in St. Andrews, which looks out over the
Old Course along the southern end of its western boundary.
We were on the edge of the right fairway at the 17th hole—the
Road Hole, it's called, because the green is mashed right up
next to a road that runs along the south edge of the property.
Straight ahead, running side by side, are the 1st and 18th fair-
ways—a big, wide, smooth, green carpet. Winding across the
fairways, just beyond the 18th tee box and just in front of the
1st green, is a little creek, which is called a "burn" over there,
with a couple of old stone footbridges crossing it.

Way off north of the first tee is a long stretch of beach and
then St. Andrews Bay. Lining the 18th fairway on the right are
the old stone and brick buildings and church steeples of the
town. It had been a sunny, kind of blustery day, but now the
wind had died down some, and it was cooling off fast heading
into night. Directly across, due east and about two par 4s from
where we were standing, the sun was finally setting against the

face of the old clubhouse of the Royal and Ancient Golf Club
of St. Andrews, which sits just behind the first tee.

(Helluva name for a golf club, isn't it?)

Everything was so peaceful, so quiet. Me and Bud had been
out there maybe five minutes, neither of us saying much, just
taking it all in. It was so beautiful. So beautiful.

Finally, I turned to Bud: "Buddy, I own this place. I love it.
I've never felt more comfortable on a golf course in my life.
This is my home."

••••••••••••••

That's the closest I've ever come to flat-out predicting that I
was going to win a golf tournament. Golfers don't do that. Not
Jack Nicklaus. Not Tiger. Not anybody. For one thing, the
odds are always heavily against you. For another, there's the
jinx factor. But mostly, you don't want to put any extra pressure on yourself. Bad enough to come down to the last green
needing a par to hold on to a one-stroke lead. That wouldn't
be a good time to remember that you'd bragged to somebody
beforehand that you were going to kick ass and take names.
The game's tough enough without pissing off the Golf Gods.

Plus, based on the way I'd been playing, there was no good
reason to think I was going to do shit in the 1995 British
Open. Since winning the PGA Championship in 1991, when I
was named Rookie of the Year on the PGA Tour, I won two
other tournaments (the B.C. Open in 1992 and the BellSouth
Classic in 1994) and made more money than I could ever have
dreamed of. During that same period, I also missed 30 cuts in
90 starts on the PGA Tour, had two WDs and two DQs, was
suspended once (and took two months off to avoid being suspended a second time), and got fined more times than you've
had hot dinners.

And that was just the golf.

I also spent three weeks in rehab, got married, became a father, got divorced, got married again, became a father again, went on the wagon, and built up a casino debt of $3.8 million.

Going into the 1995 British Open, I was a train wreck. And yet somehow I felt pretty good about my chances.

No, I felt *really* good about my chances.

For starters, as I mentioned earlier, I loved the golf course. *Loved* it. I'm not big on golf traditions like some people. I don't get weepy because Bobby Jones made a birdie here or Walter Hagen used to drink there—bullshit like that. I don't visit golf museums and I don't know much about golf history, if you want the truth.

But there's one tradition that I do care about, and it has to do with the fact that St. Andrews is the Home of Golf. Think about that: the Home of Golf! This is where the game began, in a damned sheep pasture next to the beach in a cold, rainy, windy, corner of Scotland. All those bunkers? Caused by sheep burrowing down for protection against the wind. Eighteen holes? That's how many drinks were in the jug of whiskey those old guys took with them when they played. Golf clubs? Take a look at a shepherd's stick and think 2-iron.

I know, I know—most of that, maybe all of it, is bullshit. But I like history stories, and how the Old Course came to be is a good one. Anyway, however it happened, the Old Course at St. Andrews is still the Home of Golf.

The one problem I have with the British Open, by the way, is that they don't play the tournament there every year. Why not? Why shouldn't it have a permanent home, the way the Masters does? I say the Home of Golf ought to be the home of the British Open.

I first played the Old Course in 1993 in the Dunhill Cup,

when me, Payne Stewart, and Freddy Couples beat the British team. I was 4–0 in my matches. That's when I fell in love with the Old Course at St. Andrews.

The course is set up perfect for my game. I was hitting a draw back then, and the one thing you've got to be sure to do at the Old Course is keep it left off the tee. On the back side, especially, anything right is trouble, because of the OB fence that runs all the way down the west side of the course. Too far left, though, and maybe you're in another fairway, but that's not going to hurt you too much, because there are no trees on the course, only some bushes, and even if you're way left you have a shot at the green. There are a ton of bunkers, but back then, before they lengthened some of the par 4s, I could fly them all.

Fortunately for me, Greg "Boats" Rita, who was on my bag at the time, had been on Curtis Strange's bag at a couple of Dunhill Cups, and he knew the Old Course pretty well. Boats—everybody called him that because of his humongous feet—pretty much summed up what you needed to know about the Old Course in one sentence: "Keep it left going out, and keep it left coming home."

After the Dunhill Cup, Lee Trevino and Peter Thomson both predicted I'd win an Open at St. Andrews some year. So did Gene Sarazen. Considering how awful 1993 had been for me, that was music to my ears. And one other motivation was that Jack Nicklaus had said, "If you've won the British Open at St. Andrews you've fulfilled your golfing career." I thought then, and I think now, that anything Jack says about golf is gospel.

Playing there at St. Andrews, whether I was going to play good or not, win or miss the cut, I was happy—for the first time in two years—just to be out on a golf course. I was on

Prozac. I wasn't drinking. I was crazy worried about my gambling debts. I was looking over my shoulder. I was miserable.

Except at the Old Course.

The minute I stepped out to that first tee for a practice round, I felt right at home. I could just as well have been back in Bay Ridge. I felt like I belonged. I don't know why, exactly, but I know I felt so good about being there that I played two practice rounds. Hell, I never play two practice rounds. A lot of times I don't even play one. And it's not as if I didn't know this course and had to play practice rounds to figure it out. I just liked playing it.

The happiest four days of my life in golf were the four days of the 1995 British Open. The PGA had been such a blur, it was so fast that I didn't have time to think about what was happening. It was only later that the experience sunk in, and then it was in bits and pieces, not all at once. But the British Open was something I felt shot by shot, hole by hole, as it unfolded. It's hard to explain, and I know it may not make a lot of sense, but I call it "emotional clarity." It's not that I remember every detail physically, but more like emotionally. I can't give you shot-by-shot, but I can recall how I felt just about every minute of every day.

The fans in Scotland are the most knowledgeable in golf. You hear that from guys who've played there a lot more than I have, and I'm sure it's true. They don't clap for bad shots or even mediocre ones; they clap for *good* shots. They understand angles of approach and trajectory and club choice and whether you made a good shot or just got lucky. They know you haven't really been tested until you've played in their wind and rain.

It almost makes me wish I'd been drinking then, because I'd love to have gone to a pub and spent an evening talking golf.

If you hit a bad tee ball, British fans are not going to

applaud. In the States, on the other hand, if you just get it air-
borne and hit it 330, American fans are going to yell their
heads off; they don't give a shit where it goes.

American fans get a kick out of guys hitting it long, and a lot
of them come to party and have a good time. I've had thousands of people come up to me and say, "I don't even play the
damned game, John, but I sure love you."

Being there in St. Andrews that week brought me out of a
shell I'd crawled into since rehab. I could go out there and play
that golf course every day the rest of my life. That's how much
I love it.

The 67 I shot in the first round was the best round of competitive golf I have ever played. The wind was blowing like a
sonofabitch, and it was gusty and swirling. Every tee shot was a
navigational challenge, every putt a balancing act in which you
had to factor in wind as well as grain and break. Lose your
focus for an instant and you're looking at a big number.

Golf as it was meant to be.

I followed the 67 with a 71 in the second round, and the
wind was still so tough that nobody went really low, so I was
tied for the lead with Brad Faxon and Katsuyoshi Tomori at 6
under after 36. Ernie Els, Corey Pavin, Mark Brooks, Ben
Crenshaw, John Cook, and Costantino Rocca were bunched
right behind us at five under, and several other guys were
close. That's what happens when you have a lot of wind:
nobody's going to come along and drop a 64 on the field.
Saturday I shot 73—not great, but not terrible in a major—
and dropped to fourth place, at 211 behind Steve Elkington
(210), Rocca (209), and Michael Campbell (207).

Sunday was the windiest day yet. Campbell dropped back.
So did Elk. Ernie slipped. Rocca held steady. And so did I.
Going into the Road Hole, I had a two-shot lead over

Costantino. That's where I made the key shot of the day for me, a sand shot from the Road Hole bunker that let me save bogey.

That's right, bogey. My second shot caught the Road Hole bunker, about the last place in the world you want when you're sitting at the top of the leaderboard on the 71st hole of the British Open.

You've probably seen the Road Hole on TV. It's got a pot bunker with a 6- or 7-foot face, and even if you're far enough away from the face to try to go for the pin, you only have a narrow strip of superfast green tilted like a Ping-Pong table with two legs shorter than the others.

My playing partner, Ernie Els, was in the same damned place, and he managed to get out, so that gave me a little breath of confidence. Fortunately, in a way, my ball was too close to the face for me to even think about going for the pin, so I took my medicine: I came out nearly sideways to the fringe at the back of the green and then two-putted from 30 feet for bogey.

If I'd tried to go for the pin, I might still be in there. At the Old Course, you have to accept that sometimes bogey at the Road Hole is a good score. You just have to have the patience and judgment—two qualities I'm not exactly famous for—to accept that.

It was the best bogey of my life.

The thing that had kept me in the hunt all week was not so much my driving but the fact that I had been able to two-putt from some unbelievable places all week. There are seven double greens at St. Andrews, and man, are they huge. I remember Boats stepping off the distance on number 12, a drivable par 4, in the first round. I hit a 1-iron on the green and had a 180-foot putt. It went through about four or five different breaks.

Too far to the right or left and you're off the green. I got it to about 5 feet and made the putt for birdie. I also made a bunch of 7-footers to save par. It was the greatest putting week of my life.

At the Old Course, some of the fairways actually roll faster than the greens. The greatest thing about golf like that is that you can hit any type of shot you want—there's no such thing as a wrong shot. It's just whatever you feel comfortable with. I think that if people really want to learn to play the game of golf, to learn all the shots and find their feel, then they should spend some time on a Scottish links–type course.

You can flop it on those greens, or you can putt it from off the green, or you can punch and run a 7-iron to the flag. You've got maybe 10 different options on most holes. What was great about the week is that I realized that, hey, maybe I do have all the shots.

You need to have them to survive. That's all you can do in the British Open, especially when the wind is blowing. Now, you take the wind away, guys are going to shoot 15 to 20 under par to win like Tiger's done. If there's no wind, it's not really a British Open. I love the bad weather; I love the wind. I thrive on it.

The wind's howling and I'm punching a low 5-iron into a green from 150 yards out? Cool! When the elements are really flexing their muscles on the Old Course, par becomes a great score.

The course just never gave up; the wind blew everyday. Every shot, every putt was a fight.

On the golf course, I was putting away Otis Spunkmeyer chocolate chip muffins like they were salted peanuts. I'd have four or five for breakfast, and three or four more at the turn. They had a little place back behind the 10th tee, and Greg would go get me a bagful and I'd eat them with a Diet Coke, and go on to the back nine.

Every night that week was the same. They have a bunch of receptions, and somebody's always trying to get you to go to one party or another, but I skipped them all. Every day after playing I went back to my room, took a 20- or 30-minute bath, watched the golf on TV (at least on Thursday and Friday, when I finished early), and then had the same dinner: spaghetti and meatballs, Diet Coke, and chocolate ice cream for dessert. Then in bed by 9:30 and up by 6:30.

Boring? Yeah, I guess, but I'll take boring any day at St. Andrews.

. . . .

Everybody talks about Costantino's flub on 18, and then his 70-foot miracle putt from the Valley of Sin to send us into a playoff, but most people forget the brilliant save he made at the Road Hole just before. He'd knocked the second shot over the damn green at 17 onto the path that runs between the green and a stone wall. They've got some nasty grass going up on the bank towards the wall, and he's in that shit, but then he plays this amazing putt that bounces over the road and onto the green, and he makes par. Nine out of ten times you're going to make five or six from there, maybe worse, because it would be easy for a chip from there to run right off the green into the bunker. I only saw it on TV reruns, but it had to be one of the shots of the week.

So as he's walking to the 18th tee, I'm coming off the green up ahead with a one-stroke lead. He hits a good drive and has a sand wedge into the green from a perfect angle. A birdie ties me, and he couldn't be in a better position to make one. Only he chili-dips his sand wedge and pooches it down into the

Valley of Sin, 70 feet from the pin. I've got a one-stroke lead, and he's looking at two putts.

Holy shit, I'm going to win the British Open!

Me and my wife Paulette and Bud and Boats are standing up behind the green over by the first tee. Paulette grabs my arm and goes, "You got it! You got it!" And I go, "It ain't over yet. You never know what could happen." I was lying, because I'm sure as hell thinking it's over, that I've got it. There's no way he's going to sink this putt. And Bud's got this big grin on his face, patting me on the back, hugging Paulette, looking all cool and calm, but I'm guessing that inside he's about to go off like a skyrocket. Only Boats looks a little stiff, like it *really* ain't over until it's over.

And then Costantino drains his 70-foot putt.

Shit!

Shit!

And then, okay, let's go loosen up. (*Shit! A 75-foot putt to send us into a four-hole playoff? You've got to be fucking kidding me!*) But I've got to stop thinking about what he just did and focus on what I've got to do: go back out there and play the way I've been playing all week. (*Shit!*) I said forget about it. That's history. (*Shit!*)

After their rounds, a few guys—Bob Estes, Corey Pavin, Mark Brooks, Brad Faxon—had stuck around up by the 18th green to watch me finish. That was great. Their staying around to congratulate me was really, really special. They didn't have to hang around. Most guys, me included, when they finish a tournament, major or not, are on the road as fast as they can. You don't win, what's the point of hanging around?

Also, a lot of guys on the Tour had lost respect for me over the past few years for some of the shit I'd done—and I can't say that I really blame them. Looking back, there's a lot I had to be ashamed of.

But there these guys were, waiting to shake my hand after I came off 18. That touched my heart. Then, when Costantino sank that putt to force the playoff, they were all going, "You can do it, Big Guy. Go out there and bring that sonofabitch home." No American had won the British since Mark Calcavecchia in 1989, and they were pulling for me.

The playoff was pretty much over before it even started. I made a good par on one and Costantino three-putted for bogey. On two, I made a snake from about 35 feet, over a ridge, breaking all over, that dropped for birdie. He made par. I was up two going to the Road Hole.

Here's where Nicklaus, sitting up in the telecast booth said, "Oh, gosh. Oh, no. Don't hit driver."

Sorry, Jack. As the saying goes, I was going home with what brung me. I had got a two-shot lead. The wind was howling out of the right at about 30 or 40 miles an hour. To the right beyond the tee box on 17 there's a wall, about 15 feet high, with a sign that says ST. ANDREWS OLD COURSE HOTEL. They built it to replace an old train shed that used to sit there. You've got to start your tee shot over the sign because if you start it left, you'll go into this long, thick rough that's tougher than 10-years-to-life. And if you are able to get a club on the ball and try to go for the green from that angle, you're a lead-pipe cinch to end up in the Road Hole.

Boatsie wanted me to hit 3-iron. And I said, "Remember yesterday? We hit one-iron and made six." (He had the good sense not to remind me that almost an hour earlier I'd hit driver and gone way too far left, which led to the bogey that made this whole playoff thing necessary. As if I could forget.)

At the Road Hole, you've got to get it far enough right to stay out of the gunch and you've got to hit it long enough to make sure you don't have to hold the green with anything more then an 8-iron. So I said, "Fuck it, man. I'm hitting driver. I'm hitting right over the L." That is, I was going to draw it over the L in HOTEL and let the wind push it out into the fairway.

Risky? You bet. Get double-crossed and it goes right and OB. Draw it too much and the wind would put me into the left rough again, and from there the final resting place of your next shot is almost certainly the most famous bunker in golf. Been there, done that already that day.

I hit it perfect, 330 yards, right to the neck of the fairway, an open alley to the green with the Road Hole bunker all but out of play. That left me with 139 to the hole. A little into the short rough, but a clean lie. I drew a little knockdown 9-iron to the right side of the green that kicked a little left and checked up at about 12 feet. I knew I had won the tournament, even before I two-putted for par, because Rocca was in the bunker. He ended up making seven, so I went into the 18th with a five-stroke lead.

At 18, I hit 2-iron. This wasn't the time to be a show-off and try to drive the green, which would have been a piece of cake with the wind behind me. So I hit 2-iron, walked over the famous bridge there, and stopped and waved at the fans, who were cheering their heads off. Then I gave them a windmill arm wave and they lost it completely.

At the British Open, if you're in the last group and leading the tournament coming up to the 18th green, the marshals drop the ropes and let the gallery march in behind you. It's a great, great feeling. Halfway up the fairway, I was semisurrounded by cheering, happy people. It's like I had my own personal escort.

Minutes later, after I putted out for my par and shook Costantino's hand, and when me and my posse were done hugging and kissing and jumping around like idiots, Bud got a call from Wilson and Reebok, my two biggest sponsors at the time. They wanted me to get back down to Swilcan Bridge as soon as I could. They had photographers all lined up and ready to go, and they wanted to get pictures of me on the bridge with the Royal & Ancient clubhouse in the background. But they wanted me, like, *right now*, because the light was only going to be good for a little while longer.

Swilcan Bridge is the bridge that crosses the creek—sorry, Swilcan Burn—that runs across the 1st and 18th fairways. It's like 500 years old or something, and is one of the most famous spots in golf. On Friday, Arnold Palmer, who was making his last appearance in a British Open, stopped on that bridge to wave one last goodbye. Just last summer, Jack Nicklaus did the same thing.

But before I could go down for the photo shoot, me and Costantino had to submit our scorecards, and then there was the presentation of the Claret Jug on the 18th green, and I had to say something without bawling like a baby. So by the time we finished everything, the sun was dropping, and the Wilson and Reebok people were going nuts.

So Bud and I hustled over to a golf cart and started out for Swilcan Bridge, when all of a sudden somebody came running out of the media room yelling "Stop! You got to come back! You got to come back! The President's on the phone! He wants to talk to you!"

My first thought is, holy shit, the President of the United States wants to talk to me. But then Bud pointed out that Wilson and Reebok were putting about $4 million a year in my pocket, and all Clinton was doing was taking 40 percent of that away, and that the sun was just about to sink behind the Old Course Hotel. It was now or never for the commemorative photo. So, talk to Clinton or pose for the photo? It didn't take me long to figure out what to do: "Hit it, Bud."

We get the photo shoot done with about a minute to spare.

Later that night, when we got back to our rooms in the Old Course Hotel, there were a bunch of new messages, including one that said: "Please call the President of the United States."

Fine, I said. I get the picture, and I will. But I still haven't had dinner yet, and I'm starving. Besides, I didn't even vote for the guy. But now Bud's going the other way: "He's the president, John. You've got to talk to him. Please! Do it now."

So I'm like, okay, okay, get him on the horn, only that turned out to take a lot of back-and-forth, one guy talking to another guy who told me to hold on, all this even though he'd been the one to call me in the first place. But finally a guy came on and said, "John, this is President Clinton."

Sure it was—I recognized the voice right off. You can take the boy out of Arkansas, but you can't take the Arkansas out of the boy. And so I said, "Thanks for calling. Sorry it took me a while to get back to you." And then we went back and forth a little: how do you feel, were you blown away when Rocca made that putt, you made us all proud, blah-blah-blah. And about then I recalled something: "Say, do you remember that time we played golf after I won the PGA and you were still governor? Well, you told me you'd look into a speeding ticket I got that time outside of Fort Smith the month before, only you didn't, and it's costing me two grand a year on my insurance."

So he laughed this big laugh, and said he's sorry, but he can't do anything about it now because he's not governor anymore. And then he congratulated me again, and we shot the shit some more, and I thanked him, and we said goodbye.

It was pretty nice, if you think about it. After all, here's the President of the United States, a fellow Arkansas boy, calling to say he's proud of me for winning a damned golf tournament.

(Pretty nice, but I didn't vote for him the second time around either.)

That night, as you can probably imagine, I celebrated pretty hard. But not with Jack Daniels. And not with Miller Lite.

I celebrated with chocolate ice cream with chocolate sauce, served up in the Claret Jug.

It was the best food I had ever eaten in my life.

SIX

○ ○ ○ ○ ○ ○

THE HARDER YOU FALL

I started drinking again in August 1996 in Sweden.

At the British Open that year, I played like a defending champion the first three rounds—70-73-69—then threw up all over my shirt in the final round: 77. What the hell, I still had some nice appearance-fee checks to cash at tournaments in Europe, which is why I found myself in Sweden yielding to temptation.

Since I came out of rehab, my agents always told the hotel staff wherever we were traveling to make sure all the alcohol was removed from the minibar in my suite before we arrived. Out of sight, out of mind—I was cool with that. This time, the hotel staff forgot to do it, because I discovered when I went to get a Diet Coke that the damned thing was fully stocked with beer and booze.

That night, I drank five beers. I can't even remember what kind. I was by myself, and I got hammered, because European beer is a lot stronger than American beer.

And because I hadn't had a drop of alcohol for four years.

. . . .

Back up a little. It took a while to get from winning the British Open in 1995, to falling off the wagon in 1996, to drinking myself senseless at the Players Championship, losing my Wilson and Reebok sponsorships, and spending 30 days in the Betty Ford Center, all in the space of six weeks in 1997.

So let's rewind the tape . . .

The first major thing me and my crew did after I won at St. Andrews was shave our heads. The Monday before the tournament began, I'd bet Bud, Blake, Donnie, and Mike Boylan of Wilson, who'd become a good friend, that if I won the thing, we were all going to shave our heads. They said, sure, fine, whatever you say, John. Much as they believed in me, though, I don't think any of them thought they were going to have to be going to a barbershop anytime soon.

Hey, I was as serious about that as I was about the new Mercedes I told a car dealer friend back in Memphis to have in his showcase and ready to roll for me if I won.

Sure enough, the next day after the British, by the time Blake had to get to the airport to return home, me and him were bald as billiards. But nobody had to go to a barbershop: I shaved Blake, and Blake shaved me. Mike and Donnie, they chickened out. And Bud, he must have thought he dodged the bullet, because we raced off to Holland for a tournament before I could do him, and we both spent the week running full-speed, me playing golf and basking in the glory of being British Open champion, and Bud shaking and baking, talking deals with what seemed like everybody in the world of golf.

By now, Bud probably figured I'd forgotten about the bet.

No way. On Sunday night, at 2:30 A.M., about eight hours before we were scheduled to leave for Sweden and another tournament, I knocked on Bud's door—with scissors, a can of shaving cream, and a razor on a tray. *Room service!*

I returned to the States in August to play the PGA, but I needn't have bothered: 76-73—cut. That pretty much set the tone for the rest of my regular season: 30th, T-67th, cut, T-67th, WD.

I can't say that I particularly gave a shit. I was the 1995 British Open champion. Anything else that came my way that year was pure gravy. And there was a lot of that.

....

Any notion I might have had coming out of the gate at the top of my game in 1996 now that I had my second major got knocked in a cocked hat by mid-May: five missed cuts in my first 10 tournaments. The summer wasn't much better than the spring. I did make seven straight cuts and had the best U.S. Open of my career (T-27), but I had only one top 10 finish (T-10 at the Kemper).

That's what I had to look back on when I sat down in front of that loaded minibar in Sweden.

On Friday night, after the second round of the tournament, I called one of my agents, who was in Sweden with me at the time and asked him to come up to my suite to have dinner.

"You're playing great, John," he said as he walked in the door. "This could be what turns you around. You could win this thing."

"Thanks, man, I think so, too," I said. "But sit down. There's something I want to tell you."

Then I went over to the fridge, pulled out a beer, and popped it open.

"No! No! No!" was all he could say.

And then I told him.

"Johnny, I had five when we got here on Tuesday. I didn't have any Wednesday night because I had an early tee time yesterday. Thursday night, here by myself, I drank six or seven."

He looked like he was in shock. He didn't ream me out or get mad or anything, but I know my drinking again—even if it was only beer—really, really hurt him.

I finished T-18 in the tournament. I played really good. If I'd made a few more putts, I could have won the thing. It was my best finish of the year.

But what I was proudest of that week was that I told John the truth. I didn't hide what I'd done. I could have gone on like that, sneak-drinking by myself, for I don't know how long. I could have become a closet drunk. And then I probably *would* have become an alcoholic.

My philosophy then, and my philosophy now, is that "it is what it is." You do what you do, and you accept responsibility for it. Anything else, and you're just fooling yourself. Anything else, and you're not a man.

Back home, starting with the PGA, I picked up where I'd left off: I missed the cut in my first four tournaments. After a month like that, it was pretty clear that my decent finish in Sweden hadn't meant a damned thing.

But the beers I drank there, they did.

Rumors started flying all over the place about me being seen drinking in public, which I had been, so in October my agents put out a statement over my name:

It is true that I have had a few beers on several occasions this summer, but I have not been involved in any alcohol-related incidents. I have not been drinking to excess, and this has not been the reason the level of my play lately has been below my usual standards. In fact, I have put more time and effort into my golf game than I have at any time in the past.

Back home in Dardanelle, my buddies were like, thank God, we got our John back. They meant that in a positive, support- ive way. They wanted me to be me. Their main concern was "What are you drinking? Are you drinking whiskey?"

I told them, "No way, man. I'll never drink that shit again."

Even then, I knew that "never" is a word I should probably never use. The truth is, since coming out of rehab that first time in 1993, I've had maybe 40 or 50 mixed drinks with whiskey, and I never drank all of them. I don't like the taste or even the smell of it now. I'm not going to say I'll never drink it again, but I'll tell you this: as of right now, this minute, I do not like the stuff.

The following year, 1997, started off sweet: four of my five rounds at the Hope were in the 60s and I finished seventh. Then everything went sour: two missed cuts and three middle- of-the-pack finishes in my next five tournaments. Then came the shit storm at the Players Championship.

For almost two years, me and my wife Paulette had been splitting up and getting back together, splitting up and getting back together. The only constant in our relationship was the fighting. I was miserable and pissed off all the time. Was I drinking? Hell, yes. That was the only way I could stay sane.

When we went to Ponte Vedra Beach for the Players, every- thing came to a head. She wouldn't come out on the course with me. She didn't want to have anything to do with me. And at bedtime, none of that either. Then I went out and shot a fucking 76 in the first round. And it wasn't even one of those "if I'd made a putt here, a putt there" 76s. It was a pig-ugly 76, and I was pissed.

So I grab Donnie and I go out drinking. Remember those "40 or 50 drinks of whiskey since my first rehab" I mentioned? Well, I drank a big bunch of 7&7s that Thursday night, so maybe the 40 or 50 number is a little light.

After a while, Donnie couldn't stand watching it anymore, so he left me with a bunch of caddies and told them to bring me home. We ended up at a joint called Sloppy Joe's. All told, I had been drinking for a good 12 hours. I was absolutely trashed, as drunk as I'd ever been in my life and still be standing. That night was the first time I got up on a stage and sang "Knockin' on Heaven's Door."

Finally, at about three o'clock in the morning, the guys got me back to the hotel, and as I was coming in the front door of our suite, I stumbled and crashed against this door leading into the kitchen. Smashed the hell out of it, fell down, and blacked out.

Next thing I know, I'm sprawled out on the floor, and Olin Browne, one of my good friends on the Tour, is trying to help me get up. There are five or six security guards standing around, but there wasn't anything for me to do besides watching Ollie try to haul my drunk ass off the floor. And Paulette's yelling, "Oh, my God! He destroyed the room!" And Ollie's looking at her, saying, "Hey, it's just a door."

Right, it was just a door. I've destroyed rooms before. I know what they look like after I'm done with them. This was no big fucking deal.

With Ollie's help, I managed to get up, get myself into the bedroom, and fall into bed, where I blacked out again, this time with my eyes open. (I'd done that before. I guess it must look pretty scary.)

By then somebody called an ambulance, which I didn't think I needed: I had a blackout, that's all. But the EMTs came and strapped me to a gurney and started wheeling me out. Ollie was still there, and a couple of cops now, and the security guards, and Donnie.

Then Fuzzy Zoeller came up as they were wheeling me down the hall towards the elevator. He leaned down and said, "Are you alright, kid? Are you gonna be okay?"

And I said, "No, Fuzz, I'm not. I'm fixing to lose my wife, and I ain't playing worth a shit, and I'm drunk all the time, and I wish somebody would just kill me. Why don't you grab that cop's gun and just fucking kill me. I can't live like this anymore."

At least that's what Fuzzy later told me I said. By then I was sort of going in and out, and I don't remember so good.

The first faces I saw when I woke up in the damned hospital belonged to my agents, Bud and John, and to Donnie. Paulette had gone back to Memphis, Donnie said. She hadn't even come to the hospital to see how I was. She went straight home to file for a divorce.

I told the guys I was miserable and that I had to go somewhere and see if I really needed help.

. . . .

So I went to the Betty Ford Center. I made the decision to go there on my own. This time, going into rehab really was voluntary. I went there because I wanted to, not to please the PGA Tour or anybody else. I did it for myself, to answer some questions about myself.

I almost didn't get there. I was on the highway, heading towards Palm Springs, and I started thinking, "Why bother?" My life had turned to shit. Almost a year of fighting with Paulette, and now she was leaving me. Wilson had dropped me. Reebok had dropped me. My golf game sucked. I was miserable.

Why not just drive off a cliff somewhere and be done with it?

The last time I felt this bad, back in 1992 after I destroyed my house in Colorado, I called Donnie Crabtree from my car and he talked me off the ledge. This time I called Hollywood Henderson, because of all the people I knew, he'd come closest to the place I was at right then. Thank God I got through to him.

"Big John, I can't tell you I haven't thought about ending it myself," he told me. "But think about your kids, and think about all the fans you'd disappoint if you killed yourself."

You know, I probably wouldn't have done anything. I was feeling low and shit, but I'd felt low before. I was just in one of those places where I needed to hear somebody I trusted and respected tell me that I was worth something, that I mattered to people, that I had a lot to live for. I was feeling pretty damned sorry for myself, and I needed some love. Hollywood gave it to me then the way Donnie had done five years before.

As I told Bob Verdi in *Golf Digest* a year ago, Betty Ford turned out not to be so much about the drinking as it was about learning to look in the mirror and finding something I liked.

For 30 days, I was in an outpatient program at Betty Ford. You go in Monday through Friday from six in the morning to nine or ten at night. You're there a lot of hours, but you're on your own. I had a condo in Palm Springs, so it was perfect.

Except for one thing: I went to Betty Ford blaming myself for Paulette divorcing me, and trying to figure out what I could do to get her back. But in the time I was there, I realized that when you wrote down the pros and cons of the relationship, there was a lot more negatives than positives.

I came out of Betty Ford as a stronger human being for realizing that.

There were group discussion sessions, with 10 or 12 people, men and women, all of us trying to define things for ourselves. You learned about everybody else's problems. And you learned that some of your problems were a little bigger than somebody else's, and some weren't.

But I really didn't pay attention to other people's problems, except when they were crying or something, and you wanted to give them a hug.

There was one girl in there that had been abused by her husband. So I'm going to myself, "I ain't done that one. I have never done that one." And there was another one in there whose husband was cheating on her big-time.

The best thing to come out of my time in Betty Ford was that I met Mr. Ely Callaway of Callaway Golf.

My two main sponsors, Wilson and Reebok, had dropped me while I was in rehab. The Wilson deal paid me several million a year plus bonuses, and there was five more years to go in the original contract. And I'd just done another five-year deal with Reebok.

The day they dropped me was April 28, 1997—my 31st birthday. Happy fucking birthday to you guys, too.

Mr. Callaway called me during my third week at Betty Ford. He wanted to come see me. He came out to my place in Palm Springs, and I cooked him dinner: chicken, mashed potatoes, a salad, store-bought rolls.

Anyway, Mr. Callaway said, "John, we want to sign you. Can you get your shit straight?"

I said to him, "Dad"—I called him Dad right off the bat—"I can't sit here and tell you that I'm never going to drink again. But with Wilson and Reebok dropping me, I'm not getting any quarterly endorsement payments anymore. I've got no money. My golf game sucks. I owe two or three million dollars to the casinos. My wife's divorcing me, which means I'll probably be looking at some more alimony. I'm generally screwed six ways to Sunday. So hell, yes—I'd love to sign with you."

Well, after I got out of Betty Ford, I went to see Mr. Callaway at his company's headquarters in Carlsbad, California. I met all the staff there. Great, great people. I love them to death. My agents worked out a good deal with them. The terms were great: Callaway paid off my gambling debt, which was $1.7 million, and they paid me a base salary of $1.2 million, with a bonus package based on how I played. I would switch to their clubs, of course, which was fine by me, because I always liked the Big Bertha.

But there were two conditions: no drinking and no gambling.

Mr. Callaway was a great man. A *great* man. If it had still been his private company, if it wasn't publicly traded, I think I might still be with them today. There was a lot of alcoholism in his family. He and I talked a lot about it. I think he understood what I was struggling with.

That first time I came out of rehab, out of Sierra Tucson, I had said, "I'll never drink again." Those are heavy words. They felt right at the time. But what they do is they set you up for failure if you fuck up. And people fuck up. I know.

This time, when I left Betty Ford, I said, "There's no way I'm going to tell anybody that I'm never going to drink again." That's because you still want to take it day to day, the way the program teaches you. But my whole life right then was trying to get Paulette back, get new sponsors, and get back on the Tour.

The conditions of my new Callaway contract were absolutely clear about two things: no gambling and no drinking. Fine. My responsibility. I accept it. I know the consequences. But there were all sorts of other things that, over time, wore me down.

First and worst were the medications that I was put on. I hated the way Prozac made me feel—made me *not* feel, really—when I was on it before. And here I go again.

My doctor at the time, I'm sure he was good and meant

well, but he had me on everything at one time or other. Switching me up every other month. Prozac. Paxil. Lithium. Other stuff I can't remember. And whatever he said, Mr. Callaway supported.

But doing all those medications, I got to where I thought I was losing my mind. At the 1998 Greater Vancouver Open, I got the shakes so bad I thought I was going to die. It was a warm, sunny day, and I had on two jackets, and I was shaking so bad I could barely hold a club in my hands. Corey Pavin and David Frost, who I was paired with, were great. They were more worried about me than they were about how they were playing. It was a frightening, frightening day.

Your mind can get to a point, I believe, where it's going every which way, you're thinking about too many things all at once to focus on one. You've got so many thoughts, positive and negative, whirling around inside your head that your body just shuts down. It's like it's telling you, "Hey, cut this shit out. Just stop thinking."

(Three years ago, at the 84 Lumber Classic, I had another attack like that. This time it wasn't antidepressants. This time it was stress and anxiety, nerves and tension, brought on by all the legal troubles my wife and her family were caught up in at the time. And I didn't drink enough water on the golf course; I think dehydration is what it was more than anything.)

I came out strong in 1998: two fourths and three other top 20s in my first seven tournaments. Through the Masters, I had made $368,000 in 10 tournaments. But then everything turned to shit again: in the next 15 events, I made $26,000.

Unfortunately, 1999 picked up where 1998 left off. I had no top 10s and only three top 25s the whole year. I ended up 158th on the money list, with $186,000.

If it hadn't been for my Callaway deal, I'd probably have had to declare bankruptcy. And the Callaway deal was just about to go away.

. . . .

The medications I was on were making me feel terrible. I had diarrhea all the time. I had headaches all the time. I was bloated all the time. I was jumpy and wired, then sluggish and lazy. I didn't want to have sex. I'd call them and say, "This ain't the right one." And they'd put me on another one. Just as bad. I was feeling like shit all the time.

Then there was the whole "Team Daly" thing. I didn't know they called themselves that until later, but they were this group of people—a nutritionist, an exercise therapist, a psychologist, a counselor for this, a counselor for that, I don't even know how many altogether—who kept calling me all the time and having me come in for a conference and telling me what to do. There was no ignoring them either; if they didn't get a callback, they'd just keep hounding my ass. I guess they figured that I was off on a bender or something. They meant well, and they were smart and decent people, but they were pushing me and poking me all the time to the point I felt like some kind of caged animal, being made to do tricks.

Finally, my doctor put me on lithium. That was the worst. Two days later, I was back in Palm Springs, playing some golf for fun at Indian Wells. I'm throwing up like every five minutes. I'm sick as a dog.

And I called them and I go, "There's no way y'all are going to keep me on this shit."

And they go, "Well, just try it. Be patient. You've got to stay on it."

Well, I finally looked in the mirror one day late that summer and said, "Fuck the money. I'm killing myself taking this shit." I really was. I was trying to stay on medication for the wrong reasons. For money. To keep a contract, so I could make a living.

But I knew I wasn't going to make a lot of money in the future if I kept going the way I was going. I wasn't drinking. I wasn't gambling. I wasn't playing golf worth a shit. I had split up with my wife. I didn't have anybody in my life I cared about except my kids and my parents, and I couldn't stand to have them see me the way I was.

The medications were destroying me. My cheeks were fat and bloated and splotchy. I didn't know where my moods were going to swing next. None of my clothes fit. I couldn't stand the way I felt and looked. And my golf game had turned to shit. I was a fat freak who could hit a golf ball a mile. That was it.

And I hated myself.

They say that antidepressants are supposed to level out your emotions. Well, I wasn't a depressed person until I started taking that shit.

Look, with antidepressants I'd sometimes get headaches and diarrhea, and lose my sex drive, and all kinds of shit like that. But the worst thing is they sometimes made me more depressed. That's right. They made me more depressed than I was. I'd just kind of like be "out there." I'd be kind of floating around like I was half dead.

That's no way to live. A person's got to be able to get fired up for something. Me, I've got to have adrenaline flowing when I play golf. I can't live my life like a zombie.

I had been watching my whole life just vanish. No emotions. No adrenaline. When I step on the first tee of a tournament, my butterflies need to be flapping their wings. But on this medication, I couldn't wait until the round was over.

Athletes can't live that way.

The next toughest thing, besides living with the medication, was the rumors that would flow around about where I was and what I was doing. Somebody from Callaway once heard that I was in Vegas for two or three days and that I'd lost $2 or $3 million. I'd been home practicing, getting ready for a golf tournament.

Rumors flared up about me drinking, too. I'd be overseas, and somebody would say that I was at a bar in Alabama or something. The Callaway guys were calling me every other week to check up on me. I was trying to play golf, and they were always pestering me about some new rumor they'd heard.

Finally, I just couldn't take it anymore.

I looked in that mirror and I said to myself, "I'm going to get my life back. I'm getting off this shit. I'm going to drink if I feel like it. I'm going to gamble if I feel like it. And I'm going to start playing golf. I've tried everybody else's way. Now I'm going to try my way."

And so I drove to Vegas one day in early September and I gambled a little, and I drank a little, and just as I figured, somebody called the Callaway people and told them. That was okay: I was going to tell them myself as soon as I was done having a little fun.

The way I analyzed it, the years 1991, 1992, 1993, 1994, and 1995 weren't bad years in terms of golf. I won four tournaments, two of them majors. I had a chance to win a few others. I made a lot of money. And I drank when I wanted to, and I gambled when I wanted to. Yeah, I owed a lot of money to casinos, but I was making a lot of money, and not once during those years (or later) did I ever fail to pay my gambling debts.

That's just the way I am. That's the way I live. That's the way I was going to be from now on.

I had stopped being me.

I was going to be me again.

Somebody doesn't like that?

Go fuck yourself.

After I got back from Vegas, I drove down to the Callaway offices in Carlsbad to have it out with them. Everybody's there. My agents, Bud and John. Donnie. The Callaway people. Donnie said to me, "You need to stay on the medications. You need to stay here with Callaway."

I looked at every one of them, and I said, "I love you guys. But I'd rather kill myself drinking a fifth of Jack Daniels a day, and be happy about it, than sit here and take these antidepressant sonofabitches where I feel like I'm dead anyway. Y'all can drop me or whatever. But that's it."

So the Callaway people—"Team Daly"—said they wanted me to go to a rehab center they thought would help. And because they were trying to do the right thing by me, and because I also knew that no way, no how, was I going back on those fucking antidepressants, I said okay, I'll go, I'll try it.

The clinic was in Palm Springs. Leslie, the girl I was dating at the time, went with me. She went to the women's side, and I went to the men's side. We stayed there exactly one night. I saw a bag of cocaine come over the fence. They wouldn't let me have any Diet Coke, but they're letting cocaine come over the fence? One guy tells me, "Man, we can get anything we want here. What do you like to do?"

Leslie and I left the next morning.

As we were driving away, I called Mr. Callaway to tell him my decision.

"Turn around, John," he said. "Go back."

I told him, "Mr. C., I just can't do that. I love you, and I love your company, but it's over."

He said again, "Go back, John. Turn around and go back."

I kept on driving.

At a time when other people were deserting me right and left—Wilson, Reebok, Paulette—Mr. Callaway had extended a helping hand. He saved me from financial ruin. He showed faith in me. And he did everything in his power to help me.

I loved Mr. Callaway. But I just had to do it my way. It wasn't against him or his people or anything. I just couldn't go down a path that I knew would eventually destroy me.

I know the "Team Daly" people at Callaway were trying to help. I know they thought they were doing the right things for me. And I love them for it. But I couldn't take what they were doing to me anymore.

I was not a depressed person. I was *not* a depressed person. I was being treated with powerful antidepressants, which may have been great for a depressed person, but I was not a depressed person. Not then, not now.

I also don't believe I was ever an alcoholic. I never wanted to believe that I was an alcoholic, and now I don't believe that I'm an alcoholic. What I believe, after going through Betty Ford, and thinking about it for a lot of years, is that yeah, sure, I've drunk too much too many times. But is that the same thing as being an alcoholic? I don't think so.

I can tell you this: I've destroyed more shit sober than I have drunk. Out of pure, blind anger. Shit builds up inside me, and I lose my mind. I go nuts.

My anger is worse than alcohol any day.

○ ○ ○ ○ ○ ○

SEVEN

"ALL MY EXES WEAR ROLEXES"

That's the title of a song on the CD I cut, *My Life,* to raise money for the Make-A-Wish Foundation. The music is borrowed from the great George Strait ("All My Exes Live in Texas") and the lyrics were whipped up by my old pal Johnny Lee. Go to johndaly.com and get yourself a copy. The money goes to a great cause, and I can tell you for sure that "All My Exes Wear Rolexes" fits my marital history to a tee.

I love women, I really do. I guess it shows, what with me being married now four times. But I got to tell you, it ain't been easy. I pay a few hundred grand a year in alimony and child support. I've had three divorces: one peaceful but long, one long and nasty, one short and brutal. Still, while I'm not exactly an oil painting, women do seem to like me okay. And one of my main sponsors is Hooters, so how bad could I be?

But it ain't been easy, brother.

It ain't been easy.

Dale

I met Dale in the summer of 1987 at the bar of the Holiday Inn in Blytheville, Arkansas, up near the Missouri border. I was 21, and I'd just won the Arkansas Men's Stroke Play, a tournament run by the Arkansas State Golf Association, and I wanted to celebrate.

My old friend and sometimes coach Rick Ross had been with me most of that summer, carrying my bag some and helping me figure things out. It wasn't actually your usual coach-student deal, not then and not later. A "lesson" with Rick would be him talking to me for five minutes or so, then me going to work it out. I'd already decided to turn pro at the Missouri Open in August, and I knew I had a lot of work to do. Rick's the nearest thing I've ever had to a regular coach, and I owe him a lot—not the least of which was that I pretty much tore Arkansas up that summer, winning five ASGA events and locking up Arkansas Player of the Year for the second straight year. I also won the Missouri Open in my debut as a pro.

(Thanks, Rick. I owe you a lot, brother.)

But back to Dale. I'd gone to the Holiday Inn bar because it was the only place in town I could find that was open. We started talking. She was a hand model living in Memphis, and she was home visiting her parents. We had a few drinks, we danced a little, and the next thing you know, we're a couple.

Funny thing, she was three or four years older than me, but our birthdays were on the same day: April 28. I've always believed shit like that means something.

Me and Dale started hanging out together, and she traveled some with me to ASGA tour events, and pretty soon we were living together in an apartment in Little Rock. By now we're in love, so we decided to get married. It was a big-ass wedding, because I knew that's what she wanted. And we moved to Blytheville to a house her grandparents give us. I didn't much like the idea of people giving me anything, especially not a house, but I was trying to make her happy, she wanted to be close to her family, so Blytheville it was.

I'd just turned pro, and I'd done real good at first. But I'd missed the cut in the final stage of the 1987 Q-School, so instead of spending 1988 playing on the PGA Tour and winning a lot of money and seeing the country in style, it was going to be scrimping around the minitour circuit, playing before nobody, and trying to figure out how to get gas money to drive to the next stop. That being the case, I guess it didn't really matter all that much where we lived, because I was going to be on the road most of the time anyway.

Dale went out with me some on the minitour circuit at first, which I really liked for her to do because it gets plenty lonely out there, driving from town to town every week, staying in one shithole motel after the other. But that slowed down pretty quick. I wasn't making much money, because there wasn't that much money to be made, even when I played well. She stopped going with me, and so a lot of times when I was by myself I'd end up sleeping in my car in the parking lot of whatever golf course the tournament was being played at. It wasn't a damned glamorous life, I'll tell you. And I got to doing a lot of drinking by myself, just like in college, only not so much.

Then all of a sudden me and Dale just got cold with each other. We had a lot of fun together before we got married. We drank beer together. We danced together. But I swear, something happened when we got married.

That fall, after I'd missed the cut again at Q-School, I made plans to go to South Africa, and I asked Dale to go with me.

She wouldn't. I kind of pretended to beg her. She said no. She said she didn't want to be away from her family that long, but I think it had more to do with her not wanting to be with me all that long. Whatever. What was certain is that things had changed between us. Sure enough, she started divorce proceedings while I was gone.

Me and Dale never got to where we hated each other. There wasn't any meanness between us, no big fights or anything like that. Her not wanting to have sex with me hurt. And she got to nagging me pretty hard about my drinking. The truth is, though, I was drinking pretty hard, because my golf game sucked. But mainly, me and Dale just drifted away from each other, to the point that we weren't hardly talking to each other at all.

Shit, we were living in two different worlds—literally. She was living in Blytheville, and I was living mostly on the road, trying to get my game together and trying to figure out why I wasn't already out on the PGA Tour, where I believed in my heart I belonged.

At the end of the day, it was a lot like most first marriages, I think. We were too young, too inexperienced. We didn't know how to go about living with somebody else, and we weren't clear in our own minds what we were looking for in another person to share our life with. I think that's pretty common.

We parted as friends. She stayed in Blytheville, and I moved to Memphis. We were only married about a year, but the divorce took an extra year after that to go through. I got word that it was final in February 1990 while I was playing in South Africa. No alimony. She didn't ask for any, which was a good thing, because I sure as hell couldn't afford to pay her any.

Ending the marriage was something we both wanted. Even so, in a situation like that, whether you're happy it's over or whatever, it still hurts. The day I heard the divorce was final, I celebrated by getting shit-faced drunk, losing a bunch of money in the casino, and trashing my hotel room. If you can call that "celebrating." So, yeah, I guess it did hurt a little more than I thought at the time, because I usually don't destroy things unless I'm mad about something.

We haven't stayed in touch or anything, but last I heard she's married and has a couple kids and is happy. I hope so. I think it's one of those deals where if I was to see Dale again, it would be like, a big hug and "Hey, how you doing? Everything going good?" What I'm saying is that it didn't end up as a hate thing between us.

Dale was the only one of my exes who didn't get a Rolex.

Bettye

I met Bettye in Macon, Georgia, in April 1990 at the Macon Open, one of the stops on the Hogan Tour. She was in convention sales for a big hotel chain—a good job, paying decent money. She was working at the golf course that week. We got together at the clubhouse bar after I came off the practice range.

It was a case of sex at first sight.

I'm not kidding. It's hard to imagine any two people having sex more often than me and Bettye. I want to have sex three or four times a day. I mean, I'm horny all the time. But Bettye's the first woman I've ever met up until now who liked sex as much as me. (Well, *almost* as much.)

We found this out about each other right away. That week we had a huge rain delay, and what happens in situations like that, a player has to call in to the tournament office to get status reports—are we in, are we out, when will we know for sure? I was staying about 15 or 20 minutes away, and I called every 10 or 15 minutes. You'd think the tournament officials would have a telephone list and inform the players what was what, but they wanted you to call them. So I did, over and over, until finally I was told it would be at least an hour. Fine, so I called back in 30 minutes, and I was told it would be another hour. Fine. So I called back in 30 minutes and I was told, sorry, you missed your tee time—DQ.

Missed my tee time! Shit, it was hard enough to scrape out a living on the Hogan Tour—it cost about a grand a week just to live and get from one event to another—without being out of a tournament before I ever got in. But at least there was one upside to this screwup: I got to spend the rest of the week in the sack with Bettye.

At the time, Bettye was living there in Macon in a friend's house. So I just moved in for the remainder of the week, most of which we spent in bed. But hey, isn't that the best way to get to know somebody fast?

Bettye played serious tennis and softball, and she knew firsthand about the competitive edge in sports. She'd been a college cheerleader, she had a college degree, and she was making good money. She'd been married before, just like me. And she was five years older than me, at 29.

Or so she said.

Bettye traveled with me on the Hogan Tour and sometimes caddied for me. I won once and finished ninth on the Hogan Tour money list, which got me into the final stage of the 1990 Q-School at the PGA West course in La Quinta, California. That's where I won my PGA Tour card for the 1991 season.

Those first months of 1991 were great between me and Bettye. In January, I made my debut as a member of the PGA

Grippin' and rippin' on the 6th hole at Arnold Palmer's
Bay Hill Invitational in Orlando in 2005. This is where I
made an 18 in 1998. But I've made a few birdies there, too.

Dardanelle High School, Class of 1984. This is one of the few times in my life that I ever wore a tie.

In 1974, Ol' No. 22 went to the Superdome in New Orleans to represent the Saints in the regionals of Punt-Pass-Kick, 8-Year-Old Division.

Me in the fifth grade. No logos!

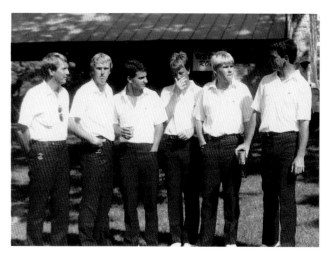

Ooooo, Pig! Soooie! The University of
Arkansas golf team in 1985.
Recognize me?

To this day, I practice hitting
wedges one-handed to
strengthen my left arm and
develop feel.

Me and Fuzzy Zoeller, my best buddy on the PGA Tour.

President Ford, Bob Hope, Vice President Quayle,
and yours truly at the 1992 Hope Chrysler Classic.

Me with my boyhood idol,
Jack Nicklaus, at the British
Open at St. Andrews in 2000.

That's Mark O'Meara without a hat on the right, and that's me
on the left. Anybody recognize the young guy in the middle?

Fighting my way out of the Road Hole bunker at the Old Course in St. Andrews in the final round of the 1995 British Open.

J.D. CUBAN/GETTY IMAGES

The Claret Cup and the 1995 British Open Champion at Swilcan Bridge. This is the picture that kept the White House on hold.

With Mom and Dad at home in Dardanelle after I won the 1995 British Open.

Sometimes you just feel like throwing something.

Another missed birdie.

Peter Van Der Reit, my caddy and good buddy,
wants to be damned sure I pull the right club.

Man, we have *got* to do something about slow play.

My daughter, Shynah, wasn't all that impressed by the Claret Cup.

. . . and the Lion shall lie down with the Bear.

Pickin' and singin' in my home on the road before the 2002 U.S. Open.

Golf?
Who wants to play golf
on a day like today?
Memphis, 1996.

PAUL HAWTHORNE/GETTY IMAGES

Getting ready to audition for a job with Hootie and the Blowfish in 2005. (PS: I didn't get it.)

At my charity golf tournaments, people give a lot of money to good causes and I get to sing and play. I like that arrangement.

Some things I just can't live without.

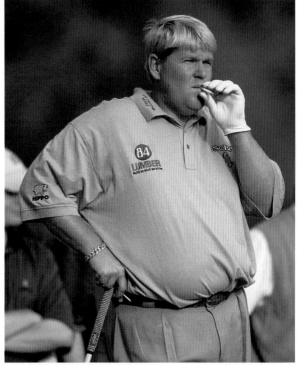

JOHN BIEVER/SPORTS ILLUSTRATED PICTURES

BILL FRAKES/SPORTS ILLUSTRATED PICTURES

Back in the day, I would go through fifteen to twenty packs of M&M's in a round. (With peanuts, please.)

In and out of trouble—again.

This is one line I *never* mind standing in.

Little John, my wife Sherrie, and me after the most important win of my career, at the 2004 Buick Invitation in La Jolla, California.

I lost in a playoff to Vijay at the Buick Open in 2004, but my son Austin made the hurt go away.

The Lion and the Tiger squared off in a playoff at the WGC
American Express Championship in San Francisco in 2005.
The Tiger won. This time.

Tour at the Northern Telecom in Tucson. My childhood dream had come true, and Bettye was with me. I didn't make the cut, but we were in love.

Our best single day together came on Masters Sunday in 1991. I had played that morning in the final round of the Deposit Guaranty Golf Classic in Hattiesburg, Mississippi, an event they used to schedule the same week as the Masters for guys like me who hadn't qualified. I shot an ugly 78 after going 68-71-68 in the first three rounds, so I was in a foul, hateful mood. That changed pretty quick, though, because me and Bettye laid up in bed and watched the whole last round of the Masters with the sound turned off, listening to Randy Travis and screwing like crazy. All told, we did it 10 times that day.

For me, it was a personal record.

(Ian Woosnam won the Masters that year when Tom Watson made double bogey and José María Olazábal made bogey on the 72nd hole and Woosie made par.)

We'd been talking about a trip to Vegas for a while, so after I missed the cut at the Buick Classic the second week of June, we finally went. I'd played seven straight weeks, missed four cuts, and needed a break. Bettye figured I was going to spend most of my time partying and gambling, and I was. But I had another item on my agenda: I wanted to get married.

Why not? I loved her, she loved me. We'd been getting along great for almost a year. Our sex life was fantastic. There was this cute little chapel right there on the Strip where we could do it without a lot of fuss and bother. So why *not* get married? But when we got to Vegas, and I brought up the idea, Bettye started hemming and hawing.

I didn't get it. Later, I found out why she said no. But I didn't get it then. Finally, I said, "We're coming back here for the Las Vegas Invitational in October? What about then?

How about us getting married then?" And she said, "Yes, John! Yes! We'll get married here in October!"

So that was it. I figured I'd be leaving Vegas with a new wife. I figured wrong. But at least I was leaving with a new fiancée.

Only then, after the PGA Championship in August, everything between me and Bettye got turned upside down.

Here's what came out over the next six weeks: it turned out Bettye wasn't 29 when we met the year before, but more like 38 or 39; it turned out she had a 13-year-old son from her first marriage that I'd never heard about; and it turned out she wasn't divorced at all but was still married to her second husband!

Some of my buddies had kind of half-joked to me before about Bettye's age. They didn't believe she was 29. I just told them to fuck off. But now, with our pictures in all the newspapers and magazines, people who knew her from back-when got in touch with people I really trusted and told them who and what she really was. All of a sudden, I went from living out a beautiful dream to fighting my way through a nightmare.

I was trying to play golf and take care of business and deal with all the great new opportunities that were pouring in, while at the same time trying to make sense of all this shit about Bettye and her past. She denied everything, and said it was all a pack of lies that my friends were spreading because they hated her.

I didn't know who or what to believe.

But I did know one thing: we had to postpone that sweet October wedding in Vegas that we'd agreed to back in June until I could sort out who she really was.

I was busy that fall with all the Silly Season stuff, but as soon as I had a little stretch of free time, I sat Bettye down back in Memphis to get to the bottom of all this shit with her once and for all.

Or tried to.

Bettye kept saying it was all a pack of lies, that this was some sort of plot to split us up. But I showed her this picture from her 1972 high school yearbook that I'd gotten my hands on, which meant that for her to be 30 now, she'd have had to graduate from high school when she was about 12. She admitted she might have shaved a few years off her age: "Don't all women do that?" she said. I reminded her she skipped an invitation to the White House to meet President Bush Sr. because her passport number hadn't matched up or something. And what about this son of hers? Did he exist or not? If he did, how come she hadn't ever mentioned him once in the year and a half we'd been together? And was she still married or what?

Trust her? Why should I?

That December I went to Jamaica to play in the Johnnie Walker Classic. I wanted to go by myself to clear my head, but Bettye insisted that she come, too. She came. Needless to say, I played like shit. I had a 77 in the first round, and a Doesn't Matter in the second, because I mistakenly put down a five on the 18th hole when I had a four and signed my scorecard without correcting it. That meant an automatic DQ.

By the time I got home, I'd figured out what me and Bettye had to do: split up.

So before Christmas, I told her to pack up her shit and get out. I told her I was going back to Dardanelle to be with people I loved—and trusted. And then she dropped the P-bomb on me: she told me she was pregnant.

My first reaction? Bullshit. By then I knew she'd been lying to me about just about everything else in her life—why wouldn't she be lying about this? It's true, she said. Prove it, I said. (Shit, she didn't look pregnant. She looked as good as ever. But, as it turned out, she was about four months gone.)

So that was pretty much that—I thought. I went to Dardanelle; she packed up and moved out of our house in Memphis. It was done with. We weren't even married; we were just two people splitting up. No harm, no foul. Only she didn't go back home to Macon or whatever. She got on a plane and flew to L.A. and hooked up with that famous "palimony" lawyer, Marvin Mitchelson.

(Oh, and one other thing: on January 6, 1992, her divorce from the guy she'd denied even existed finally became final.)

We were done with each other except for one little problem: we still loved each other. Or maybe not. I do know we still liked having sex with each other as much as ever. And we had fun partying together. But I also realize, looking back, that we weren't best friends, the way I believe two people who truly love each other should be. Friendship is based on trust and sharing. But I knew I couldn't trust her, and as for sharing—well, I think Bettye was committed to my business, if you know what I mean. The money was pouring in, and—although it didn't really penetrate my thick skull back then—it's now pretty obvious to me that she wanted to make sure she got plenty of it.

You know, it's so funny, before I married her, it was like all fun and games, and all she wanted to do was be there for me. (Bettye caddied for me, for God's sake.) But as soon as we got married, it was like, she wanted to run my life, no ifs, ands, or buts.

Anyway, Marvin Mitchelson fired off a letter to me saying that I had until January 24 to reach an agreement with his client—that is, cough up a bunch of money—or she'd take my ass to court with a palimony suit. My response was a printable version of "Go fuck yourselves." Here's what I told some newspaper: "It's sad. It's hard to believe that someone could be that crooked, that mean. It makes me look stupid. Here I go with this girl for a year and a half and I didn't know how old she really was or that she had a kid or that she was still married."

Maybe they thought I was going to roll over and play dead or something. But I was righteously pissed off, and I wasn't going to be bullied into paying her off, given all the grief she'd put me through. So she filed suit, asking for a million dollars and all kinds of other shit, and I went off to Australia to play some golf and make some money. I won the Australian Skins, but my heart wasn't in it, and after an 81 in the second round at the Australian Masters, I didn't sign my scorecard and got DQed.

And when I got home, guess what? Bettye had withdrawn her lawsuit because Tennessee didn't recognize palimony. Me and Bettye were back to square one.

So we got married.

That's not as crazy as it sounds. Bettye was pregnant, remember. And we hadn't figured anything out, and she was due in June. At least all our shit was finally out in the open—or at least I hoped it was. And we both wanted the kid to be, you know, legitimate. So we went to Vegas in May and got married. And in June, our daughter, Shynah, was born.

That summer, I planned to play in the Federal Express–St. Jude Classic in Memphis, like I always do, only this time my mind wasn't on golf, and I withdrew. Instead, I became a father for the first time.

That's right. We'd scheduled a C-section for June 10, the day before the tournament began. (That's one way to get out of the pro-am!) So that Wednesday morning, me, Mom, Dad, Jamie, and Don Cline went to the hospital.

Oh, and Bettye came, too. (Just kidding!)

When we got there, they took Bettye away to get her ready. Me, I'm in the waiting room pacing around like a madman and smoking like a factory—you know, just like your average first-time father-to-be. Finally—it seemed like hours later, but it probably wasn't—a nurse comes out and says they're ready for me, and hands me this green scrub suit and tells me to put it on. Uh-uh, I say. No way, I'm not going in there. But this nurse is pretty clearly used to getting her way. Put this on and follow me.

Much to everybody's surprise, especially my own, I did what she said—for once, I actually did what somebody else told me to do—and I can only thank God that I did. I stood up at the head of the bed holding Bettye's hand during the delivery. And after they got our new daughter, Shynah, all cleaned up, I got to hold her. I cried like a baby. I'd never seen anything so beautiful. Somebody took this dopey picture of me holding her, this shit-eating grin on my face, the proud poppa.

It was one of the three most magical moments of my life, the other two being the births of my daughter Sierra and my son, John Patrick Daly II. I was in the delivery room for all of them. New life coming into the world—that's a miracle, pure and simple. There is nothing like it, nothing like seeing new life come into being, nothing like it in the world.

And I'd never have known it if I hadn't listened to that tough-ass nurse.

Oh, and get this: Shynah was born on June 10—make that 6/10—at 6:10 in the afternoon and she weighed 6 pounds, 10 ounces. I don't play roulette, but if I did, you can guess my lucky numbers.

I think I know what you're thinking: mine and Bettye's little story sounds like some bad soap opera, especially when you look at the highlights:

- December 1991: Right after Christmas, I tell Bettye to pack up and move out.

- January 1992: Me and Bettye get back together, just after her divorce to the guy I never knew she was married to in the first place.

- May: We get married in Vegas.

- June: Our daughter Shynah is born.

- August: We buy a house in Colorado.

- October–November: We sort of split up.

- Early December: Bettye persuades me to come back and spend our first Christmas with Shynah.

- Later in December: I destroy the Colorado house.

- January 1993: I go to rehab at Sierra Tucson for 18 days. Me and Bettye have—I think this is the right term for it—"conjugal visits" while I'm in treatment.

- March: We buy a new house in Isleworth, Florida.

- July: I file for a divorce. (But it doesn't become final until January 1995.)

Can you believe all that?

No wonder my golf game went to hell in 1992 and 1993.

The divorce took a year and a half. We were only married a year, but she got real greedy, because now I had so much guaranteed money coming in from big sponsorship deals with Wilson and Reebok. We did it through a mediator instead of going to court. I wish now I'd taken her to court because she wouldn't have gotten a dime, what with all her lies and shit. Whatever, I've been paying a ton of money every month ever since Shynah was one year old. Don't get me wrong: I don't mind paying child support—Shynah's my baby, and there is nothing I wouldn't do for her. But something tells me much of the money benefits Bettye.

Fact is, I had so much money that I didn't care. I wanted to get it over with, and she was smart. Bettye knew how impatient I can be, and she knew how deeply I cared about our daughter. She had me by the balls, and she knew it.

Boy, did she squeeze.

And yes, she left with a Rolex.

Paulette

I met Paulette at the Bob Hope Chrysler Classic in Palm Springs in January 1992. I was in a foursome with Bob Hope, former president Gerald Ford, and Vice President Dan Quayle. (Not bad company for a 25-year-old hell-raising college dropout from Arkansas.) We were standing on the tee box of the 10th hole at Bermuda Dunes, waiting to tee off, when I saw her.

She was Classic.

What I mean is, she was one of the three Hope girls who followed Mr. Hope around at his tournament. They're always these gorgeous women in shorts and T-shirts with either Hope or Chrysler or Classic written across the front. That day, with play so slow, the way it always is at the Hope, they just kind of hung out with us, and clapped when Mr. Hope hit his tee shot, and went and fetched cheeseburgers and Cokes for us. For me, mostly. All day long, they'd bring me cheeseburgers when I got hungry, which was . . . well, pretty much all day.

And I was so damned hungover I was chugging Diet Cokes like they were beers.

Like I said, Paulette was Classic. She was also absolutely drop-dead beautiful. I couldn't take my eyes off her. But I got all shy for some reason. We made eye contact, but mostly all I did all day was just look at her. The first Hope girl I actually spoke to was Hope, whose real name was Danielle, and who turned out to be one of Paulette's friends at the time. I asked her, "Do you think she'd go out with me?" She said, "I'll ask her." She did, and me and Paulette started talking a little bit. We went out the next couple of nights there in Palm Springs.

She was 19 at the time. She lived in an apartment in Palm Springs. She was trying to be a model, but was working at the California Pizza Kitchen. (They make good pizza.) When I left that weekend—I missed the cut, by the way—I tried to get her to come with me to Phoenix, but she couldn't. We saw each other now and then, but we didn't really get together until the following summer, after me and Bettye had finally split up.

We got along great right out of the box. I mean, she was really, really beautiful. I had a bus for traveling between tournaments, and she went with me everywhere. Six months later, when my divorce from Bettye was finally done with, I missed the cut in Phoenix and I said, "Let's go to Vegas and get married." She said okay. Just like that.

So we drove up to Vegas and got married on January 28, 1995, at the Little Church of the West on the Strip, just down from Bally's, my favorite casino hotel in Vegas. I didn't want to have a big wedding, but Paulette, she invited what seemed like everybody she knew in California. Hey, that was okay—it was my third wedding, but it was only her first, so why shouldn't she live it up?

We had a nice honeymoon in Bally's—I lost a bunch of money, but at the time I didn't care—and everything was cool. I bought her a Rolex.

That was the summer I won the British Open, of course, and everything was great. At least for a while. But after Sierra was born on June 1, 1995, it just kind of went downhill between me and Paulette. There was something missing between us. Paulette had 14 hours of labor with Sierra, and afterwards she began missing California, missing her mom, not caring so much about being with me.

That hurt a lot, but what hurt as much, maybe even more, was her not wanting to travel as much. She wanted to stay in Palm Springs all the time. She really didn't like it in Memphis, even though I built us a beautiful new home right on the TPC Southwind course. It's still one of the nicest homes I've ever owned. It was beautiful. But Paulette wanted to live in California, Plus, she didn't want to travel with me except to "the good places."

Things always seem to start going downhill when I get married. With Paulette, it got to where she only liked to go to the "nice" tournaments. She didn't want to go to the ones that weren't so fun for her. At first, she loved my bus. After six months or so, she hated it. And she missed her mom, too. She was so young.

Thing is, though, I'm on the road so much that I need my family to be with me. I've always wanted to have someone with me. I've never really been without a woman. In college I was, I guess. But when I turned pro it was Dale, and then

Bettye, and then Paulette. Plus, when I was on the road by myself and single, I always made sure I wasn't exactly by myself, if you know what I mean.

I'd started drinking again in the summer of 1996, and pretty soon it was getting bad for me. Because here I was, married to this gorgeous woman, who turned heads every time she walked into a room, but after Sierra was born, we'd go like five or six days without having sex. We had ourselves a situation, no two ways about it.

One night, probably around 11 o'clock, in our new place in Memphis, I said, "I see we're out of milk again. I'm going out to get some." And I came back three days later. I drove down to Tunica and spent three days gambling at the Horseshoe, looking for a little peace of mind.

All the women that I've been married to, they all know that I play golf, that I gamble, and that all I want besides plenty of lovin' is Diet Coke in the refrigerator and a clean house. And I do most of the cleaning anyway. I'm a neat freak.

What's the problem with that?

They know who I am. They know what I do. It hasn't changed since the PGA, except for the booze. For me, it's golf and gambling. I'm a homebody. I don't do anything. I don't ever want to go out. I hate going out to eat. I never want to go anywhere unless it's a casino. It's the way I was when I met them, it's the way I was when we were together, it's the way I was when we split up, and it's the way I'm going to be tomorrow.

What's so hard to understand?

I just got the sense from Paulette that she didn't want me around. I just think she felt like maybe she made a mistake in her life, marrying me too soon. Or whatever. But it's got me thinking that maybe she was in it for the money. I got her out of a stupid job. Actually, I shouldn't say stupid. The California Pizza Kitchen's got good food. But I took her away from that. I took care of her and we had a baby together. I was totally in love with her, madly in love with her. It was probably the way she looked more than anything. She was a sweet, soft-spoken woman. You wouldn't think she'd have a mean bone in her body.

But boy, when it got time to get a divorce, holy shit!

It wasn't long and delayed and drawn out, like it was with Bettye, but it wasn't easy either. The thing in Ponte Vedra Beach at the 1997 Players Championship, where she accused me of destroying our hotel room, that was the worst, because all I did was fall into a door to the kitchen and smash it in. Bust up our room? No way. Bust up our marriage? Well, it didn't take much by then.

That was when I went off to the Betty Ford Center on my own.

Paulette filed divorce papers on me soon after I got out.

She got her Rolex and a lot more.

Almost Ex No. 4

I met Almost Ex No. 4—let's call her Leslie—in the lobby of the Four Seasons hotel in Austin in October 1998. The Four Seasons in Austin is a great hotel. It's right on Town Lake, dead south of the state capitol, and just before dark, you can sit out back and watch about five million bats fly out from under this bridge where they sleep during the day. It's really weird, but it's great.

I was doing an outing down there for Duck Soup. They

used to be like the official band of the PGA Tour—a cover band that played at just about all our stops back in the 1990s, only not so much anymore. I was good friends with them. So one day Sam, the lead singer, called up and asked me, "You want to come to Austin for a little bit of money?" I said, "Damned right. I need it. Yeah, I'll be there."

Anyway, it was sort of a strange night in Austin. I was upstairs in my room with another girl I'd met, one of these one-night-stand things. And I got this call from Sam, "There's a girl downstairs who really wants to meet you, man. You need to come down here and meet this girl right now." And I said, "Sammy, I got a girl up here right now." And he said, "Just come down for a little bit. Tell the one you're with you're going to take a walk."

Well, I went down and Sam introduced me to this girl and I'm like, "Good God almighty!" She had this tight skirt on and a low-cut blouse. Young and gorgeous. Young and *gorgeous!* I found out later that she was a former hurdler and very athletic. She worked out all the time, just a complete workout nut. Dark complexion, beautiful body, kind of auburn hair, and just out-of-this-world gorgeous.

Hel-lo, Leslie. Pleased to meet you.

We talked for a little bit, and we swapped cell numbers, and a couple of weeks later I called her and asked her to come out to Palm Springs for the Shark Shootout. (I had to explain to her that the Shark Shootout was Greg Norman's great Silly Season tournament.) She flew out to California—she'd never flown first class before—and we spent some time in Palm Springs, and then went on to the Shootout, and she enjoyed it a lot.

We were together for the next two years.

Now, the interesting thing about Leslie was that she liked

girls as much as she liked guys, if you know what I mean. She loved wine, and she liked to come out and watch me play golf. She was the total package.

And a beautiful package it was.

She also loved to hang out at titty bars. A lot of men are going to think this was another dream come true, but let me tell you, it cost me a lot of money to take her to those joints. I mean, she would get more lap dances than I would.

At the 2000 Masters, I shot 80–73 and missed the cut, but I had to do a charity event with Hootie & the Blowfish somewhere real close to Augusta the following Monday. So me and Leslie decided to hang around town for the weekend. Some guy had rented an entire big bar downtown for the week, and he'd brought down a bunch of strippers from Atlanta to entertain the guests. So naturally, we go down to check it out.

There's this huge room, with a dance stage and couches, and a big, long bar, and I say, "Can I get a private room? My girl-friend wants a private room. Just bring three or four girls down."

Well, we get the room, and the next thing I know, Leslie's naked as a jaybird except for high-heel shoes, and she's danc-ing on this pole as they wheel in all this beer and liquor for all my buddies that are coming to the party.

Then these two girls come into the room, and Leslie gets one of them over on the couch, and she starts . . . well, all I'm going to say is that she was having a good time, and so was I. After a while, Leslie brings the next girl over, and it's the same deal. This goes on for like four or five hours. We all got ham-mered and had a great time.

When I go out to settle, the place is jammed with people partying hard. I make my way to the bar, and this old country boy down at the end hollers out, "Hey, Daly—man, I wish you'd have made the cut." I tell him, thank you, brother, and ask the guy in charge to tote up my bill.

The guy at the end of the bar, he's drunk out of his mind, really having a good time, and he says, "I got your bill, buddy. I got your tab. Don't worry about it." I tell him, "Brother, you don't want my tab. We've been here a while. We've had probably twenty dancers. There's no telling what I owe." The guy goes, "Naw, fuck it, it's on me." And they start toting up the bill. "You do *not* want this bill," I say again to the guy. "Thanks, but this is a big 'un, and you really shouldn't." He goes, "Oh, fuck it, man. I love you, John. I'll take care of it."

By now, Leslie's just laughing her butt off, and I'm like, I don't want to cause a big scene by not letting this guy do what he wants to do. Finally, the guy who's running the joint goes over to the old country boy with the bill and says, "That'll be $9,700." Now the old country boy kind of flinches, and he looks at his buddy, and he looks at the bill, studying it, and finally he says, "Fuck it. Put it on my credit card." And one last time I say, "No, no, man—you don't have to. Just buy me a beer or something." And he says, "Please, John. I want to."

And so I let him pay the damned bill.

Me and Leslie, we had us some really good times. She was really something when it came to sex. She was always ready to go out and party. She liked to travel with me. She got along with my friends. She watched pretty much every round of golf I played while we were together. Plus, she stuck up for me.

One time I was playing some tournament, and she was standing beside the green while I was waiting to putt. A couple of drunks come up and stand next to her, not knowing who she was or anything, and one nudges the other, nods towards me, and semiwhispers, "Can you imagine anyone fucking that?" Leslie, she turns around and says, "Hey, pal—you think they call him 'Long John' just because of his driver?"

Now *there's* a woman standing up for her man.

Eventually, I proposed to Leslie mainly as an excuse to get her a five-carat engagement ring, because she wanted one after two years together, and she wouldn't get off of me about it. That's okay in a way, because she deserved one as much as, if not more than, the others. But on the other hand, I should've never done it, because I really never planned on marrying Leslie. I loved all the fun we had together and stuff, but marriage was never on my mind.

Leslie was a semester and a little from getting her degree, so in the summer of 2001 she went back to college to take some courses, with the plan to finish up in the fall. I bought her a car, and I got her an apartment. (I'd already got her a Rolex.) I told her, go back and get your degree and stay out of them damn titty bars.

Things might have worked out for us, at least for a little while longer, except for one thing:

That summer, on June 10, 2001, in Memphis, Tennessee, I met Sherrie Allison Miller.

○ ○ ○ ○ ○ ○

EIGHT

THE DALY NUMBERS

They count everything on the PGA Tour. It's gone way beyond the obvious stuff: stroke average, driving distance, number of putts, that sort of thing. They keep tabs on how many times a guy follows a bogey with a birdie (bounceback). They calculate how you rank on putts 3 feet and under, right rough tendency, scrambling from the rough, shit like that. They tabulate the number of up-and-downs everybody has, birdie conversion percentage, and proximity of the hole. How many times does a guy hit the Port-A-San? I bet the Tour office can tell you.

At the end of the day, of course, the most important stat is scoring average. Top that list at the end of the season and it means you (a) won a pile of money, (b) won some tournaments, and (c) get to keep the Vardon Trophy for a year.

The second most important stat, and the one that determines how you do on the first one, is putting. Finish in the top 10 in putting and you've had a great year, period.

But there are all sorts of other numbers that, taken together, tell you a lot about a pro golfer—about who he is as well as how he's doing.

For instance:

62

The lowest score I ever had in a PGA Tour event came in the second round of the Invensys Classic at Las Vegas in 2001. A lot of guys went low that week, because my four other rounds were pretty good, too—67, 72, 69, 67—and I only finished T-7. Won $130,000. Pretty sure I left it all in Vegas, and then some.

87

The highest score I ever posted in a PGA Tour event came in the third round of the Bay Hill Invitational in 2000. I'd rather not discuss it.

18

Q: John, how did you ever make an *18* on the 6th hole at Bay Hill in 1998?

A: Well, I missed a 3-footer coming back for 17.

Bet you've heard that one before, because Arnold Palmer once used it to explain an 11, and Tom Watson used it to explain a 14. Hey, we all make big numbers now and then. Sometimes because of bad breaks, sometimes because of bad shots, sometimes because of bad judgment—and sometimes because of all three. My 18, which came at Arnold's tournament, the Bay Hill Invitational, back in 1998, was a classic.

I'll tell you how I made it. You tell me whether it was bad breaks, bad shots, bad judgment—or all three.

The 6th hole at Bay Hill is a dogleg left par 5 that bends 543 yards around a lake. The standard approach is to take the water out of play on your drive, lay up with a 5-iron or something, get it close with a wedge, and make your putt for a birdie. Worst-case scenario, you make par.

Worst-case scenario? Naah, that would be what I did.

See, I was two under for the tournament at the time and I was thinking eagle all the way to move up on the leaderboard. That required cutting the corner of the lake and getting myself close enough to go for the green with a mid-iron. That was the plan, at least. Instead, I shaved it too close and got wet. Okay, no problem. I'll just go up about 50 yards to the drop zone, cut a big 3-wood over the corner of the lake onto the fairway, hit my fourth shot close, and save par.

Let me say right here what I said back then after my round: this was a good plan, and I had the shot to make it happen. It was a smart play.

Splash!

Shit! Now I'm hitting five, in the same spot because I started the ball over the water. Forget eagle, forget saving par, forget moving up on the leaderboard. But I *have* that shot.

Splash!

Splash!

Splash!

Splash!

Thunk—solid ground at last (13). Well, sort of solid: I was buried in a bunker.

Sand wedge out to fairway (14).

Six-iron to greenside bunker (15).

Sand wedge to 25 feet (16).

Two putts (17, 18).

(By the way, I birdied the next hole.)

Needless to say, I was dragged off to the media center after the round to explain to reporters how I made the 18. (You'll be proud to know that I spared them the joke.) Here's what I said:

It wasn't that I didn't care. I just lost my patience. I was determined. I knew I had the shot. I had the courage to try it. I just didn't have the wisdom to bail out. The way I look at it, it's progress before perfection. I'm not going to worry about it. I just got a hell of a lot of practice with my 3-wood.

Tom Watson, one of my playing partners, called it "a comedy and a tragedy all in one." That's pretty accurate I guess.

Looking back, with the benefit of hindsight and the wisdom that comes with age, here's what I think: good plan, easy shot, smart play.

I did the right thing.

1

The number of my career holes in one in tournaments officially sanctioned by the PGA Tour. Hey, it's not easy: the odds against making a hole in one are about 5,000 to 1.

−12

At the 1991 PGA Championship, I played the four par 5s in 12 under. For the tournament, I shot 276—12 under. I won by three strokes. Guess you could say my distance was the key.

−2

At the 1995 British Open, I played the two par 5s in two under. For the tournament, I finished at 282—six under. I won in a playoff. Guess you could say my short game came into play.

17

The number of tacos I ate to celebrate my 17th birthday.

On April 28, 1983, the Helias High School golf team was returning to Jefferson City, Missouri, from a golf tournament, and I mentioned that it was my 17th birthday. Coach Hentges, whose son Chris played on the golf team and later went on to be an All-American running back at Iowa State, said, "Great! Congratulations! You get to pick where we stop for dinner."

Tough call. Normally back then, it would be McDonald's or Burger King, but I picked Taco Bell.

For dessert, we went next door to Burger King, where I had a double chocolate soda and a Whopper with cheese.

Happy birthday to me.

2:26

That's the time Mark Calcavecchia once took to play one round of golf.

If you're in the second group to tee off on the morning of the final round of a golf tournament, it means you played pretty average golf on Thursday and Friday to just barely make the cut and on Saturday you basically blew any chance you might have had of making any noise on Sunday. You tee off Sunday looking to just get it over with and get out of town.

That's the position me and Calc found ourselves in at the 1992 Players Championship. We were the second group to tee off that morning, and the first wasn't even a group: it was Bob Tway, who'd gone off as a single.

Now, you need to know that me and Calc, we're the two fastest players on the Tour. We were then and we are now. But we didn't go up there on the first tee and say the hell with it, let's go out and play as fast as we can. We weren't trying to catch an early plane or anything. But I asked Calc, casual-like, what do you say we try to catch Bob? He said sure, okay, whatever—and that's what we did. We caught him on the 17th hole.

We did it by hustling between holes, not taking a bunch of practice swings, and not taking forever to line up putts. But we never hit out of turn, and we tried on every shot. It wasn't like we were raking putts and loading up on seven or eights. I shot 80, and Calc shot 81. Not too shabby for two hours, twenty-six minutes.

The way I saw it, we were out of the tournament, no way we were going to make any kind of move, so why not give the fans something to enjoy? And believe me, they enjoyed it. There were about 20,000 people already out on the course, waiting for the "real" tournament to begin a couple of hours later, and once they caught on to what we were doing, they went nuts. They were cheering us as we ran past them and they were cheering as we trotted off the green and they were cheering the pretty damned good golf we both played.

You think they would have had such a good time if we'd slogged around the course, heads down, grinding away, all glum because we were so far out of the tournament? I don't. I think the people saw we were just having fun. Isn't that why they call golf a *game*? And aren't you supposed to *play* a game? Play-game-fun—get it?

Me and Calc said then, and I'll say again now, that we were in no way disrespecting the game of golf. Actually, we didn't think all that much about exactly what we were trying to do besides catch Bob Lohr, which we finally did on 16.

I remember Calc on 18 tee saying, let him try and fine me for this one. He was talking about Beman, and I said, fine us for what? Calc said, you watch, John. He's going to try to fine us for something.

But what we did wasn't a bad thing. Fans sent letters to the PGA Tour saying what a thrill it was for them to see something like that. The fans there had a good time. The fans who may have seen some of it on tape highlights—the live broadcast didn't begin until after we'd signed our cards—had a good time. Besides, if it had been me and Calc playing in a twosome for a tournament at our *normal speed* with nobody ahead of us, we would have only taken 20, maybe 25 minutes longer. As I said, we both play fast.

21.3

That's how many seconds I take over a putt on average. The average on the PGA Tour: 39.4. Look, I'm the fastest player on the Tour. Lee Trevino said he always played fast because he thought he could pull the shot off and he didn't want to have time to think about missing it. That's me all the way. When the pace slows down, I start thinking too much. It affects my putting the most. In 2004, I was one practice swing and boom. Before the 2005 season, some people put it in my head to take more time, and so I started taking two, three practice swings. In 2004 I finished fifth on the Tour in putting average. In 2005 I was 115th. See what I'm saying?

2002

That was the last year I led the PGA Tour in driving distance—and most likely the last time I ever will. That year I averaged 306.8 yards. In 2003 I added almost 8 yards (314.3) and dropped a notch, as Hank Kuehne blew past me with 321.4. Since then, young bucks like Bubba Watson and J.B.

Holmes have come on the scene, which means Ol' Long John's gonna have to be content with bumping it out there 310 and waving as they fly over. That's okay. I had me a pretty good run as the Tour's designated long-distance driver: 1991–2002.

50+

The number of times I've seen *Dead Solid Perfect*, my all-time favorite golf movie.

20+

The number of times I've seen *Caddyshack*, my second all-time favorite golf movie.

0

The number of times I was in a movie theater last year. Hey, I have two 42-inch plasma-screen TVs in my bus and a big 72-inch job in my house. Besides, where are you going to find *Dead Solid Perfect* in a movie theater at the mall these days?

32

The number of golf balls I go through in an average tournament—when I make the cut. I beat 'em up pretty good.

22/6/5

The typical number of PGA Tour events/European Tour events/Silly Season events I play over the course of a typical year.

14,600

The number of Marlboro Lights I smoke per year—two packs a day. (Okay, okay—so maybe it's really more like 18,250.) I was figuring that out with the calculator on my computer, and I remembered the time when somebody asked me after a round, how many cigarettes did you smoke today, John? I'm like, do you seriously think that I'm out on the golf course counting cigarettes? All I worry about counting on the golf course is strokes.

514
The number of gallons of Diet Coke—based on fifteen cans a day, my average—that I drink per year.

30
The average number of Monday–Tuesday golf outings and appearances I do each year.

450
The number of dollars it takes to fill the gas tank of my tour bus, which is my home on the road. I love that baby.

35,000
The number of miles I put on my tour bus every year.

Too Many
The number of trips I made to some casino or other in 2005. Figure 25 to 30. Or maybe 35 to 40. But I'm trying to cut back, honest I am.

Maybe 5—Also Too Many
The number of times I ate dinner in a sit-down restaurant in 2005. I'm a homebody. I don't ever want to go out. I hate going out to eat. I never want to go out anywhere, unless it's to a casino.

6

The number of golfers to win two majors before they turned 30: Bobby Jones, Jack Nicklaus, Tom Watson, Johnny Miller, Tiger Woods—and me. I try to think of that every time I start getting on myself for some of the bad shit I've done to myself over the years.

9

The number of golfers who had to withdraw from the tournament in the week before the 1991 PGA Championship for me to get a chance to grip it and rip it.

$30,000

The amount I donated from my 230,000 PGA Championship purse in 1991 to an educational fund for the two daughters of a man who was struck by lightning and killed on the first day of the tournament.

$55 Million

My approximate net loss at casinos in the last 15 years. It could be a little more. I know it isn't any less.

0

The number of times I'd fly commercial the rest of my life if I have anything to say about it, even if it means spending my last dime to avoid it. Hey, I don't mind the fans and signing autographs, but I hate all the other stuff about flying commercial. Get to the airport an hour and a half before departure time? Then sit on the plane for another hour while they get their shit together? Not being able to smoke? Give me my bus any day and point me towards the interstate.

$1.5 Million

That's what my bus cost me, and it was a damned good investment.

$19,200,000

The payoff for three high-roller types who supposedly put down $80K each on me at 80-to-1 in England, where betting's legal, to win the British Open in 1995.

288.9

Good for first place (by 6.6 yards) in driving distance on the PGA Tour in 1991.

288.9

Good for 97th place in driving distance on the PGA Tour in 2005.

65 (and Counting)

The number of signed guitars I have hanging on the walls of my music room in my house in Memphis. They're signed by musicians I really admire—guys like Johnny Lee, Willie Nelson, Garth Brooks, Moe Bandy, Stevie Ray Vaughan, Glen Campbell, Tom T. Hall, George Jones, Eddie Van Halen, Glenn Frey, Prince, Vince Gill, Graham Nash, Kid Rock, and B.B. King. Also by whole groups: Hootie & the Blowfish, the Rolling Stones, Guns N' Roses. Most of them, guys have given to me. A few of them, I've bought at charity auctions. Sometimes I just look at them and think of all the fine, sweet music they represent. God, I wish I could play half as good as any one of those guys.

NINE

○ ○ ○ ○ ○ ○

THE GIFT OF LOVE

No two ways about it, I'm an impulsive guy. A lot of the time—okay, most of the time—I do things based on how I feel, then think things through later. Sometimes, that doesn't work out so good, like when I used to drink too much and punch out a wall, or now, when I gamble too much. But over time, I've come to trust my feelings, because I know in my heart that I love people.

After I won the 1991 PGA, I donated $30,000 to set up an education fund for the two little girls whose father had been killed by lightning the afternoon of the first round. It wasn't that I had a whole bunch of money to be giving away back then, or that I spent a whole lot of time figuring things out.

It just seemed like the right thing to do.

Well, in the summer of 2005, I met those little girls—now young women—for the first time. Now I know for sure that what I did 15 years ago was the right thing to do.

I like helping people.

It feels natural.

· · · · · · · · · · · · · ·

A thunderstorm began to move through the area around Crooked Stick on Thursday afternoon during the first round of the 1991 PGA. When that happens at a tournament, sirens sound, play is suspended, and a fleet of carts and vans is sent out to pick up players and caddies and take them back to the clubhouse.

But how do you evacuate 35,000 spectators? You don't. They hear the sirens, of course, but they're out there on their own, many of them a long way from shelter or their cars. Some are sitting in metal bleachers, which are especially vulnerable when lightning moves into an area. Two months before Crooked Stick, a spectator was killed by a bolt of lightning at the U.S. Open at Hazeltine National Golf Club near Minneapolis.

Damned if the same thing didn't happen at Crooked Stick. I didn't become aware of it until the next day, when I read about it in the papers. A man who was seconds away from reaching his car door was hit by lightning. Actually, I think he was carrying an umbrella and that brought the lightning right to him. A couple of EMTs tried to revive him, but it was too late. An hour later, he was pronounced dead at a local hospital.

How awful is that? We're out there hitting a little white ball with a stick for millions of dollars, and this man who was only out there to watch us, support us, have some fun on a summer afternoon, gets killed by lightning.

The man's name was Tom Weaver, and he was 39 years old. That's no age to die, especially when you leave behind a wife and two young children, as Mr. Weaver did.

I was depressed about the whole thing and for some reason, I felt partly responsible. I never mentioned it to anyone, but I decided on the spot that if I won the tournament, I would do something for Mr. Weaver's two children. I'm not going to pretend that I'm a spiritual person, but I believe that God put that thought in my head. It came from my heart, and the Good Lord saw to it that I was there when the awful tragedy occurred.

When I won on Sunday, I delivered on the promise I had made to myself by donating $30,000 of my $230,000 first-place check to a trust fund to provide for the college educations of Mr. Weaver's two girls, Karen, who was 8 at the time, and Emily, who was 12.

After I made sure the money was going to be invested properly, I never attempted to contact the Weaver girls. It wasn't because I didn't care about them. I just didn't want to dredge up the awful memory of that terrible day. Imagine being so young and having to hear that news. I also never made a big deal about my contribution because that was between the girls and me. Some celebrities and athletes like to make a splash when they do something charitable, but that's not my style, and the guys I know on the PGA Tour feel the same way.

They give a lot back, but they don't beat their own drum for doing it.

Last spring, my agent received an e-mail from Steve Fisher, who identified himself as the husband of the former Dee Weaver, who he'd married in 2000. He wanted to get in touch with me to let me know about the girls. Of course, they weren't girls anymore. Karen was about to graduate from Indiana University, where she majored in biology, with plans to become a doctor. She was still living around Indianapolis. Emily was now married and living in Oswego, Illinois, near Chicago. She was about to earn her degree as a respiratory therapist from the College of DuPage.

I was really touched. Isn't it amazing what a little money can do when it's spent the right way for the right reason?

Last summer, I called Dee Fisher and introduced myself.

Dee was shocked, and almost speechless. It was pretty emotional. I told her I'd like to meet her and the girls if they wanted to meet me. We settled on the day after the PGA Championship. I was going to fly that Monday to Fuzzy's annual fund-raiser in Sellersburg, Indiana, not far from Indianapolis. Steve and Dee said they would be there, and they were going to bring Emily and Karen.

So, after 14 years, we finally got together. I was putting together an episode of *The Daly Planet*, my reality show that premiered on the Golf Channel this year, and a camera crew was in town. But I didn't want to force anything on Emily and Karen, so our first meeting was private. They gave me a big hug and thanked me over and over. They showed me their scrapbooks, which included their diplomas and the first pictures I'd ever seen of their dad.

A couple of golf magazines had published stories about the girls and me getting in touch, so it wasn't a secret or anything anymore. After we talked a bit, I asked them if they would mind being guests on one of my first shows. They said, sure. So I brought in the camera crew to tape me, Steve, Dee, Emily, and Karen talking. Then Emily and Karen said they wanted to read a letter they had written to me.

Here it is:

Dear John,

It is hard to find the words to thank you for the selfless gift you gave to us. We lost a wonderful man, our dad, that day but you stepped up to the plate, big time. When your unexpected gift was received, it was above and beyond what we could have imagined or dreamed.

We now, looking back, have a much greater appreciation for what you had to sacrifice to help ensure our future. We hope that you are proud of our accomplishments—we gave school 100 percent and along the way learned to live, laugh and love.

Please know that we will always have a special place in our hearts and we will always be eternally grateful.

Thank you and may God bless you like he has us!

Emily and Karen.

I'm not much for crying, but when Emily read that to me . . . wow!

In their letter, Emily and Karen asked God to bless me, but I told them He already had. He put me at Crooked Stick for a reason, and it wasn't just to win a golf tournament.

My gift to them was from the heart. It just came out.

I think it came from the Lord.

And I think it came from my mother, the way she raised me, and the way she always treated people.

The gift I gave them 14 years earlier could never come close to replacing their father, of course, but it did provide them the college education that he would have given them if he'd had the chance. And I've since found out that the $30,000 was invested so well that it will take care of Emily's and Karen's children, too.

To meet them and to learn how they're leading their lives, that was their gift to me.

· · · · · · · · · · · · · · ·

I play golf for a living, but I don't see it as what my life is really about. I think my life is really about people. I'm not a real religious person. My relationship with God is personal. But I think I was put here on earth for a purpose, and that purpose has to do with helping people. Everybody's always asking me, how come people love you so much? Is it because you hit a golf ball a long way? I don't think so. Maybe at first, but shit, there are a lot of guys out there now who hit the ball just as far as I do. I think people love me because they know—they feel—that I love them.

And I do.

People do things that make them feel good. When I high-five people walking from green to tee, it means as much to me as it does to them. When I give a golf ball to a kid, it makes me feel good to see his eyes light up. I love people. When I came out of a casino in Australia once after losing a bundle and gave a homeless guy on the street a thousand dollars, it was because he was broke and hungry—it felt right because he was a hell of a lot worse off than I was.

People love me. I don't know why for sure, but I think it's because they trust my feelings for them.

Last year, at the WGC AmEx in San Francisco, after I lost the playoff to Tiger Woods, I came off the green and gave my putter to this Japanese guy. He went nuts. He couldn't believe it. It was just a putter that I'd missed a 3-footer with to lose a playoff. It cost me a two-year exemption, a place in the Mercedes Championships, an extra $550,000, and another 10 spots in the World Rankings. I didn't want that putter. To hell with that putter.

But I could have broken it over my knee or thrown it in the lake or sold it on eBay or just stuck the damned thing back in my bag. (After all, the putter didn't three-putt on the first playoff hole—I did.)

Instead, I gave it to somebody and made him feel good, something I've loved doing all my life.

My point is that it's a two-way street: I give people stuff and it makes them feel good—but it makes me feel good, too.

....

Last year the PGA Tour raised $32,201,000 for charity. I'm not 100 percent sure, but I believe that's more than the NFL, the NBA, Major League Baseball, and the NHL raised *combined.*

The reason we're able to raise more than any of the other pro sports is that we're able to employ the golf pro-am as a fund-raising tool, and they can't. (Can you imagine the Pittsburgh Steelers running a pro-am? The medical bills for the "am's" would cost more than the event raised.)

But beyond the pro-ams at the official PGA Tour events, there's a bunch of tournaments run by individual golfers that raise another ton of money for charities. (That's true of football, basketball, and baseball players, too.) I'm just guessing that a third, maybe half of the guys on the PGA Tour run charity events every year. The percentage may be even higher on the Champions Tour. Some are small, local affairs. A few are big deals, with national TV contracts.

PGA Tour members are required to play in the Wednesday pro-ams at officially sanctioned tournaments. To play on Thursday, you have to play on Wednesday—that's our deal with tournament sponsors: they put up those huge purses; we play in the pro-ams.

The "official" pro-ams, to tell you the truth, don't hold a candle to the individual events we run when it comes to fun. And at the larger individual ones, there's another consideration: the pros play for nice purses.

Now let's take a look at my two favorite tournaments in the entire world: the Boys & Girls Clubs Tournament in Dardanelle, Arkansas, and the Lion's Heart Invitational, in Tunica, Mississippi.

My mother started the Boys & Girls Clubs event in 1994. Over the years, it's evolved into the best damned party in Yell County, if I do say so myself. And it raises about $60,000 a year for the Boys & Girls Clubs in the area.

The golf part of it is a two-day scramble on Saturday and Sunday with about a hundred teams that pay $100 to play. That's $100 per team, not per golfer. From the git-go, we wanted the tournament to be accessible to local people who like to play golf and want to help the Boys & Girls Clubs, but who don't have the means to pay $5,000 to $10,000 per team, like they charge at bigger, fancier events. We also raise money through sponsorships.

But the best part is the big party we throw. Over the years we've had it in big tents at my parents' place and at Chamberlyne Country Club in Danville, where we've usually held the golf tournament. This past spring it was at the Lion's Den Golf Club, formerly the Bay Ridge Golf Club, the same course I practically grew up on.

What makes it so great is that a bunch of my music friends come to the party and perform: Johnny Lee, Hootie & the Blowfish, Moe Bandy, and Billy Pierson. In recent years, a certain professional golfer who fancies himself a picker and singer has got up on the stage with them and tried not to make too big an ass out of himself.

Plenty of beer, plenty of good country food, plenty of great music, plenty of dancing, plenty of golf—how can you not have a good time?

The other tournament that will always be on my playing schedule is the Lion's Heart Invitational in Tunica, which succeeds the John Daly Make-A-Wish Foundation Tournament I hosted in Memphis. Over a dozen years, the Make-A-Wish raised about $4 to $5 million. A huge tip of my cowboy hat for helping make that successful goes to folks like Vince Gill, Johnny Lee, Hootie & the Blowfish, Amy Grant, Joe Walsh, Glenn Frey, and Mickey Gilley.

The greatest personal benefit I derived over the years from my association with the Make-A-Wish Foundation in Memphis can be summed up in two words: Lori Laird.

When I first met her, back in 1994 at the first Make-A-Wish Foundation event I got involved in, she was Lori Reed, she was 16, and she wasn't supposed to live to see 17 because of cancer.

Six months to live.

That's what Lori had to look forward to.

Well, flash forward to 2006. Lori Reed is now Lori Laird, 27 going on 28, married, with two young girls, and living in Arkansas, where she runs her own business. Last November her doctors declared her cancer-free.

Funny, she told Bob Verdi of *Golf Digest* that I taught her about how to "keep fighting when you're down." That's nice to hear, but Lori has it all turned around. *She's* the one who has inspired *me*. Lori's the only living, breathing, bona fide *miracle* I've ever met.

We still stay in touch. Whenever me and Sherrie and the kids are in the neighborhood, our boys play with her young girls. She is the most cheerful and positive human being I've ever met. She's like, "Cancer? What cancer?"

She's a fighter, and a constant source of inspiration for anybody who's lucky enough to see her smile.

As I said, I'm not religious, and I don't go to church, but I do believe God put me together with Lori. Every time I think my life sucks, every time I feel like just giving up, I think of Lori, and it helps set me straight. When I think of her, I get goose bumps.

There's a reason we met each other.

There's a reason we're both still alive and kicking.

And that reason is that God put me there for her, and God put her there for me.

The first Lion's Heart Invitational was held last October. Justin Timberlake headlined a show that helped raise $200,000. That money was distributed to various charities through the John Daly Foundation, which me and my wife created two years ago.

The Lion's Heart takes place at the Horseshoe Casino, and—like the Make-A-Wish always did—has a great group of musicians who contribute their talent to a killer party. Last year we also had a celebrity poker tournament as part of the event. (I lost some, of course, but that's okay because it was for a helluva good cause.) We have 40 foursomes at $10,000 a team, plus a bunch of really generous sponsors.

I also sponsor the Arkansas Alumni Tournament (*Ooooo, Pig! Soooie!*), help out at local charity events around my home, and support the charity tournaments run by friends of mine on the Tour.

In the future, I plan on doing even more of this kind of stuff for one simple reason: I like it.

My motto: If doing good makes you feel good, do more of it and feel even better.

○ ○ ○ ○ ○ ○

TEN

"YOU DON'T KNOW ME"

A lot of shit has been written about me over the past 15 years. And you know what? Most of it has been true. I've always got along with reporters and writers because I just tell them the truth and don't try to bullshit my way through an interview. I think they respect that, and with a handful of exceptions, they've treated me fair.

Take a guy like Bob Verdi of *Golf Digest*, for example. He's written a lot of words about me over the years, and sometimes he's come down on me pretty hard. But he's always been fair, and he's always given me a chance to tell my side of things, and he doesn't twist things around to make himself look smart. A few reporters make the story about them, and about how smart they are. Not Bob. He tells it straight. Hard sometimes, but always straight.

Other writers, like Tim Rosaforte and Rick Reilly and John Garrity and Doug Ferguson, who have covered me a lot of years, fall in that category as well: tough sometimes, but always fair. The same's true of Larry Dorman, who used to write golf for the *New York Times* before going to work for the Callaway company.

But what do you really know about me based on what you've read and heard all these years? I'm guessing it pretty much adds up to something like this: I hit the ball a long way, eat hamburgers, smoke too much, gamble way too much, used to drink a lot of Jack Daniels, get married and divorced a lot, love music, and live in a bus on the road.

Fine. That's more or less true. But if that's all you know, then like the title of a song I wrote the lyrics for, "You Don't Know Me."

You might get to know me a little better if we could sit down for a little Q&A. So let's do it. I'll do the Q—and I'll also do the A. (And if you've got your own Q for me, fire it off to johndaly.com and I'll make sure you get an A. Just keep it clean!)

Are You Still Drinking?

That's a one-part question, but let me give you a two-part answer.

1. If I was still drinking whiskey, I wouldn't be drinking anything right now. I'd be dead. That's the truth, and I know it.

2. I drink beer. Miller Lite. Sometimes just a little. Sometimes more. And sometimes—not as much I used to, but sometimes—too much.

The first time I came out of rehab, in 1993, I said I was never going to drink again. The second time I came out of rehab, in 1997, I said I would never say I was never going to drink again. Now, I just pray I never drink whiskey again, because if I do, I know it'll kill me.

But What About Your Old Friend, Jack Daniels?

Most people would be drunk for two weeks on the amount of JD I used to have before dinner. Nowadays, I don't even like the smell of whiskey. I used to drink to get drunk. High school, college, my first years on the Tour, I'd soak my problems in Jack Daniels. Not anymore.

Do You Do Drugs? Did You Ever Do Drugs?

You can't play professional golf with your brain scrambled on drugs. It just can't be done. So my answer to your first question is no, absolutely not, I do not do drugs.

Now, have I ever done drugs? Sure, in college, I smoked a little grass. Who didn't? But I never liked it. All grass did for me was make me want to eat about 25 Big Macs and go to bed. And it made me thirsty. As I told Bob Verdi last summer in *Golf Digest*, if grass makes me want to have a beer, why not just forget the grass and have the beer?

I don't need any extra incentive to have a beer.

Are You Ever Going to Stop Smoking?

Hey, I gave up whiskey, remember? You can't go expecting me to give up cigarettes, too.

What Do You Do to Stay Fit?

That's a trick question, right? Look, people are always saying how great they feel after a workout. Not me. Every time I get on a bike or a treadmill, I go puke afterwards. I try not to get within a pitching wedge of the fitness trailer they bring to tournaments. And I'm sure as hell not going to some fucking health club, because they won't let you smoke.

Last year, a bunch of us were sitting in the clubhouse after practicing, having a beer and shooting the shit, when Tiger comes through in his workout gear, on the way to the gym. I say to him, "Hey, man, don't you ever get tired of that workout shit? Why don't you just come over and have a few beers with us and hang out?" He goes, "If I had your talent, John, I wouldn't have to work out."

The way I see it is that I walk 5 miles a day, four days a week, assuming I make the cut. If that's not enough to keep me fit, then I'd better start looking for another line of work.

Why Do You Talk About Sex All the Time?

Probably because I'm thinking about sex all the time. I want to have sex two or three times a day with my wife, Sherrie. I love her. I love her body. I love her attitude. I love everything about her.

I think sex helps my golf. I swear it does. At the BMW in Germany in 2001, me and Sherrie were making love like crazy, and I won. At the 2004 Buick Invitational in San Diego, same thing, on my bus, and I won. At the WGC AmEx in San Francisco in 2005, we had sex all week, and I would have won if I could have putted worth a shit.

So whenever you see John Daly playing great golf, you know his wife's taking care of his needs. And when you see John Daly playing bad golf . . .

Look, if you think about sex as much as I do, it can get tough out there in a golf tournament. You got good-looking women all over the place. Some of them take off their underpants and sit around the greens and flash you when you come up to putt.

Women are always coming up to you in the parking lot and asking you to sign their boobs.

I used to do that a lot, hundreds of times over the years, but after that thing with Tiffany on the Internet, I don't sign tits anymore.

Who's Tiffany? What Thing with Tiffany on the Internet?

You don't know what I'm talking about? Hell, you must not have a computer. Seriously, it was all over the Internet a year or so ago. I figured everybody'd seen it by now.

Tiffany is a stripper from Canada who posted pictures of me and her on the Internet. We were both topless, and we were drinking and having fun at a party. I sued her for going public with the photos after promising before a bunch of witnesses that she wouldn't, and I won a $600,000 judgment.

What happened was this nice old guy—somebody told me he does septic tanks and sewers all over Canada—threw this big party at the Bell Canadian a couple of years ago. Nothing out of the ordinary, just a lot of women and booze and dancing. But then a girl came up behind me and grabbed my nuts, and she had her top off, and somebody took a picture. I said, "Whoa! What the hell is this? You're not using this for anything, are you?" "No, no, no," she said. "We're just having fun." There were women all over the place, partying like crazy. So I just kept taking pictures with this woman, who told me her name was Tiffany.

Then, about a year later, those pictures of me and Tiffany came out on the Internet. Sherrie went ballistic. She was absolutely convinced I'd cheated on her. I did moon the crowd one time (my big Arkansas ass is in one picture). I did sign

Tiffany's boobs. And all this shit goes out over the Internet. But there was never any sex. To this day, Sherrie thinks there was an orgy going on there, but if there was, no one invited me.

I did something wrong, getting my picture taken with half-naked women. But it's not like I'm getting in their pants or anything. We were all just having fun. And there was a couple of hundred witnesses who stated that Tiffany said she would never put this on her website or use them publicly in any way. And that's what won the lawsuit for me.

But the damned thing almost cost me a divorce.

So I made a pact with myself: never again do anything at any kind of party in front of a camera.

After all, I've got kids who surf the 'Net.

Do You Watch Much Golf on TV When You're at Home?

Golf on TV puts me to sleep. If I want to take a nap, all I have to do is lie down on the couch with a golf tournament on the TV—10 minutes later, I'm out like a light.

When I'm in Europe, it's a little different, because they show what seems like 100 times more shots than we do. In the U.S. they'll beam you into a tournament and show two or three shots, and go to commercials for two minutes. When they come back, they'll often talk about a single player, and not show a shot, then go back in to commercial.

I know commercials pay the bills, but there's got to be a way to show more golf. Too bad every tournament can't be like the Masters, with only four minutes an hour of commercials.

One other thing: they show every shot Tiger hits—good, bad, indifferent. I love Tiger to death, I really do. But the way the technology is today, there's no reason why, on Saturday and

Sundays at least, they can't show everybody who's out there playing. But everything's Tiger, Tiger, Tiger, even on those super-rare occasions when he's not playing good.

Unless you're a good golfer yourself, it's not easy to see on TV what kind of shot a guy made. They show you a swing, a tight shot of the golfer's face, and then some kind of aerial shot with the ball barely visible against the sky, and then the ball landing. But do you know how or why it got there? Usually not, because the announcers don't always tell you, and you probably don't know how to figure it out yourself.

Last year, I was watching Tiger play the Tour Championship in East Lake. I wish I'd been there, but I was sitting in the clubhouse at Bay Ridge with some buddies, watching it on TV. One time, Tiger hits this shot and before he completes his swing, I said, that ball's going right. And the guys looked at me, and they're like, how did you know it was going right? I said because you guys were watching a golf ball flying through the air. I was watching Tiger's legs at impact. His legs got a little ahead of the ball, and so he hit it right. But only a professional golfer can tell at impact, maybe 90 percent of the time, what's going to happen.

What's really helped golf on TV is the power swing analysis that they do to show why a guy missed a shot. Peter Alliss and Gary McCord use it well. Zinger and Faldo are great with it. Johnny Miller's awesome. I think it's a great tool.

To me that's why a lot of people watch golf, to see what happens when your legs get ahead of the ball a little bit, or you don't rotate your hips, or whatever. You hit it right. What happens when you lag? People don't know what lag means, you know? What they should say is, what happens when your right side is behind? You're going to hook it.

Make it simple for the viewer, but teach him something, too.

You Have Four Kids. Any Golfers Among Them?

Little John. When I'm home, all he wants to do is go outside with me and hit golf balls. If I practiced as much as he does, I'd have four majors.

What About the Others?

Right now, Shynah wants to sing and play guitar. It's too early to tell about the guitar, but she has a real pretty voice. Austin wants to be a movie star. He's a natural. Sierra is great playing with, taking care of younger kids. I see her being a teacher. Wouldn't that be something? A child of mine becoming a teacher?

Why Do You Prefer Traveling in Your Tour Bus When You Could Fly First Class Everywhere?

Because my bus is a lot more comfortable, it's more private, and it doesn't fly.

See, I don't like flying. Don't throw a bunch of statistics at me about how much safer air travel is than driving. I know that. I don't care. Obviously, a lot of times I can't avoid flying. But if I have a choice, I'll always take my bus and leave flying to the birds.

My bus is 45 feet long. It's got a Prevost engine that's strong enough to tow a car if I need a second one besides the courtesy car at the tournament. Outside, there's a a small refrigerator, a freezer, and full-size barbecue grill that folds out, along with a small TV I can watch while grilling steaks. There's also storage space for a picnic table and chairs, as well as for luggage. Some guys I know keep a motorcycle in there; another stashes a golf cart.

Inside, it's about 900 or 950 square feet, divided into two rooms. The bedroom has a California king-size bed, which is larger than your standard king. Two of the three couches in the living room make down into beds. There's a chair-recliner for me to sit in to watch one of the two 42-inch plasma TVs (and a satellite dish on the roof to make sure the picture's good and clear). Leopard-print walls, granite countertops. Full kitchen, with plenty of cabinet space. Washer-dryer. Dishwasher. Bathroom with full shower.

And no fucking workout room.

On my bus, I get to leave when I want to, come home when I want to, stop when I want to. It's cheaper (or at least no more expensive) in the long run than hotel rooms and airplane tickets and meals at restaurants (which I hate anyway). No security checks, no flight delays, no waiting forever for your luggage, no ticket screwups, no hassles if, God forbid, you should want to change your departure plans—and no "clear air turbulence" to scare the living shit out of you.

Plus, on my bus, I can smoke.

You sure you want to make a case for the 747?

What's the Skinny on Tiger?

Skinny? Have you seen the arms and shoulders on him this year? I hear he went the whole month of December without touching a club, but you can damned well bet he spent some time pumping iron.

I'd love to hang out with Tiger. We get along real good

when we see each other. But that's almost always the week of a tournament, and we're both crazy busy. As busy as I am, I got to believe he's even busier.

The rap against Tiger is that he's always so prim and proper and programmed and shit like that. And it's a bad rap. The guy is drop-dead hilarious. And he's sure as hell not a prima donna. He's the Tour's leader in the clubhouse in fines for dropping the F-bomb on live TV. Of course, it figures he'd top that list, because the TV camera's in his face just about every minute he's on the course. He can't get away with shit.

But I guess that long layoff didn't leave him all too rusty. All he did this year was start off with back-to-back wins.

What About Vijay? Don't Tell Me He's Funny?

Damned straight he is. Maybe I bring it out in him a little because I'm so loose, but we have a helluva good time riding each other, and we genuinely like each other.

Last year, when me and Veej were going head-to-head in the Shell Houston Open, I felt bad because everybody cheered when he missed a putt to send it into a playoff. (He won the tournament, of course, because I couldn't make a putt.) Afterwards, in the pressroom, somebody asked him, if he had finished ahead of me and seen the possibility of a playoff, how much time would he have needed to warm up. And he goes, I know what you're getting at, but JD never needs to warm up— he's always ready to play. Then somebody else asked if it bothered him that the fans were rooting for me so hard. And he says, "Hell, no, I root for John, too."

But the best time me and Veej had it going together was in 2004 at the Buick Classic in Flint. We're both playing lights-out golf, and we're paired on Sunday in the last group, and he's got a three-shot lead. Anyway, on the range before we tee off, I kind of chip a ball at him, and he goes, "I am going to kick your ass today." And he says it loud to make sure that everybody hears him. And I go, "Bring it on, Veej. Just bring it on."

So then we tee off, and after four holes, I've got a one-shot lead after going birdie, eagle, birdie, birdie. And he's laughing, and I'm laughing, because I'm birdieing every hole. We go at it like that all day long, me one up, then him one up, then me again. Finally, I need par at 18 to force a playoff but I make bogey, and he wins. He shakes my hand and says he's sorry anybody had to lose. You play that good, you almost don't care who wins. (Key word: almost.)

After we're done signing our cards and start heading over to the media center, Vijay says, "John, you make it all look so easy."

And I go, "Veej, I'm so used to going through divorces, losing wads of money at casinos, trying to pay bills, trying to pay taxes, trying to pay alimony, trying to keep my weight down, and taking care of kids, do you really think I've got time to worry about my golf game? Shit, golf's way the easiest part of my life."

How Much Do You Practice?

Nowhere near as much as I'd like to. When I'm on the road, playing and doing appearances and stuff, I don't have the time. At a tournament, the most I'll do is hit a few drivers to loosen up, then hit some L-wedges to get my timing tuned. But that's not practice; that's warming up.

I've never been a ball-beater. I've always been a guy who gets bored on the driving range. It doesn't mean anything;

you're just hitting them out there. I've always liked working on my short game a whole lot better. I mean, I'll sometimes hit 10 or 15 drives, then spend an hour or more chipping and pitching and putting. Sometimes I'll work a couple of hours going through my wedges, hitting one-handed, a hundred balls or so with each wedge.

One thing besides driving that I don't spend a lot of time on is putting. That's a personal thing, but for me, putting is mainly about feel, not mechanics. I can practice my stroke all day long and it won't make a damned bit of difference if I don't have a feel for it. It's hard to describe. When you've got it going, when you see the breaks and when you bring the putter head back and through without thinking consciously about how hard, it's a magical feeling. But feel's not something you can practice.

What I like best is to practice on the golf course. I'll find a hole and spend an hour hitting balls from all over. You can't do that at a tournament, obviously, and even in Dardanelle I have to wait until real late in the afternoon when the course is pretty much empty. But it's the best way by far to practice your game. You're not just hitting the ball out into a field, the way you do at a practice range. You're hitting to positions on the fairway that set up your next shot, and you're hitting at greens, and you're hitting different kinds of shots—flops, bump-and-runs, fades, draws.

When I'm home in Memphis, even though I live right on TPC Southwind, I don't want to play golf or practice golf or think about golf. I just want to play with Little John and Austin and be with Sherrie and catch my breath before I have to go back out on the road.

My best practice time is when I'm in Dardanelle. I can just walk outside to the practice range behind my house, beat wedges, putt some one-handed, practice chipping. It's real quiet. In the summertime, I can take my shirt off, something I'm damned sure not going to do if there's people around. I've even got lights up there so I can hit balls at night.

Some of my buddies will come up, and hang around and hit with me. And some days they'll let me practice on my own so I can concentrate. They say I got to win next week.

Problem is, I don't get to Dardanelle near enough anymore.

McDonald's or Burger King?

I think Burger King's got the best burgers. Wendy's burgers ain't bad. And I love McDonald's fries and their sausage biscuits. And their Quarter Pounders are good, too. But my favorite burger is the Double-Double, Animal Style, at the In-N-Out chain in California. That's two meat patties, with ketchup and mustard and pickles and onions cooked into the meat. I pitch the top half of the bun to cut down my carbs. Trust me, it's worth a trip to California.

What Else Do You Like to Eat?

I eat salad. I eat an orange or a banana every now and then. I'm not big on apples or pears or any of that shit. I love anything chocolate. I consider spaghetti and meatballs my lucky food ever since I won the British Open and ate that every night all week. Pizza. Mexican food. Mainly, I'm a meat-and-potatoes guy. Steak, well done. Baked potato with sour cream. Barbecue. I don't mind turkey. Fried chicken, but I try not to eat too many fried foods.

What About Vegetables?

I hate vegetables. I never eat them. When I was a kid, my father used to make me sit at the table until I ate the vegetables on my plate. But when I did, I puked, so he finally stopped.

Fish?

I hate fish. The last time I ate fish was a piece of fried catfish when I was seven years old. Even though I'm from Arkansas, I never learned how to fish because I absolutely, positively hate fish.

How Much Are You Weighing These Days?

Depends on which days you're talking about. Back in the middle of 2005, I stepped on the scales one day and—holy shit!—I was at 278. I don't know how in the hell I got there, because I didn't feel like I was eating that much, but there it was, and the scale wasn't lying. So I just started watching what I ate, and by Thanksgiving I was at 235. I had a six-week layoff from golf in November and December after breaking my hand in an accident, and then there was Christmas, so I gained back about 10, but by the time the U.S. Open rolls around I'll be back somewhere between 220 and 235.

No big deal. My weight can go up and down like a yo-yo. That's why I have racks of pants in my closet running from 36 inches at the waist to 44 inches. All I have to do to lose weight is to decide to lose it.

Funny, when people see me now, in person, they go, "Damn, you've lost a lot of weight." Sometimes it just looks like I have, 'cause when you see me on TV, I look 30, 40 pounds heavier. (And I look about 6 foot 7, when I'm only about 5 foot 11.)

My problem in terms of keeping the pounds off is that all I drink is beer now. Beer puts weight on me faster than whiskey.

Early to Bed, Early to Rise?

If I'm playing in a tournament, I get up really, really early. And the night before a round, I'm always in bed by eight or nine o'clock. This past winter, though, being home a lot and letting a broken hand mend, there were a few days I didn't get out of bed until two o'clock. Since I wasn't able to swing a golf club for about six weeks, I figured it would be a good time to get a little rest.

Now, if I'm partying or at a casino, my hours will be a little different.

What's Your Favorite 1995 British Open Story That Nobody's Heard?

That's tough, because I spent a solid year after winning there when it seemed like I didn't talk about anything else. But there's one very special story that began before the Open even started and ended with a celebration party that I wasn't invited to.

A couple of weeks before I left for Scotland, I called up a good friend, John Sisinni, and asked him and his family to come over for a cookout. I was taking some time off before the British, partly because I'd been playing shitty golf and partly because I was tired and felt like taking a break. I was on Prozac at the time, and that shit was just turning my system inside out. I did spend some good time practicing, which I hadn't been doing enough of, but mostly I was just kicking back, which I hadn't been doing hardly any of.

"We'd like to come over," John said, "but my dad's in town for the weekend." "So bring him along," I told John. "We'll cook some steaks and we'll hit the pool." I wasn't drinking at the time, so I wasn't going to offer any booze or beer, but I figured we could still have ourselves a good time.

Well, John brought his family, including his dad—and he brought his movie camera and filmed the whole thing. Us cooking and eating, me and his dad fooling around in the pool, a chipping contest, the works.

John's dad was a retired steelworker from Youngstown, Ohio. He took up golf late in life and had really come to love it. He and some buddies had a regular Monday golf group called the Over 80 Club. They weren't over 80 age-wise—John's dad was in his 60s—but I gather they sure as hell were over 80 golf-wise. Anyway, John told me his dad got a huge kick from hanging out with a real, live golf pro, even one who'd been playing like shit for most of the year.

But the story doesn't end there. When John sent the film to his dad back in Youngstown, he did a strange thing—he told him not to watch it, not just yet. "I don't know why," John told me later, "but I had this strange feeling, what if . . . ?"

His dad was a little disappointed, but he said, "Okay, I'll hang on to it."

Flash forward to the Monday after the British Open. The Over 80 Club has just finished playing, and everybody's talking about the tournament, and how exciting it was, and John's dad says, "Boys, let's go over to my house. I have something I want to show you, something special . . ."

I wish I could have been there.

You Got to Keep the Claret Jug for a Year. How Cool Was That?

Way cool, especially because it came as a total surprise to me. The real thing, too, not a replica—the R&A lets the winner hang on to it until the next Open championship.

Only problem is, the thing damned near gave me a heart attack.

That fall, when I finally got back to Memphis, I parked the Claret Jug next to my PGA (replica) trophy on the mantle in the office of my new house. The Jug came in this heavy, wooden, steel-banded storage box, with a lock for safekeeping, but I only put it in there when we were going to be away a few days or when I took it somewhere to show somebody.

I treated it like a beloved member of the family.

One day, my old friend Don Cline drove over from Dardanelle to visit me and Paulette. We had a nice dinner, and we spent some time admiring the Jug. The next morning, Don and I picked up the CEO of Wilson, my top sponsor, at the airport and drove up to Jackson, Tennessee, where Wilson manufactured their golf balls. We toured the plant, and then went up to the executive offices, where the top guys were going to have their pictures taken with me and the Jug.

I've got this heavy-ass box with me, and everybody's excited about seeing the oldest, grandest trophy in golf, so I make a big production out of unlocking the box and s-l-o-w-l-y opening the lid and . . . nothing.

Nothing! The damned box was empty! I almost shit my pants!

Where was the damned Claret Jug?

My first thought, insomuch as I could think at all at the time, was that somehow somebody had stolen it the night before. But how? I've got a state-of-the-art alarm system, and

we live in a gated community. What could have happened to
it? All this shit is going through my mind, including the head-
line in every paper in the world the next day: JOHN DALY
"LOSES" GOLF'S GREATEST TREASURE.

"John?" It was Dandy. "John, why don't you call home and
ask Paulette if it's there?"

Call home? Why didn't I think of that?

You guessed it. The Claret Jug was sitting right where I'd put
it during dinner the night before—on the dining room table.

You know, I still wonder, what would the R&A have done
to me if I had lost their Jug?

Does the R&A Give You a Replica of the Claret Jug to Keep When You Return the Real One?

Give? Not bloody likely, as the Brits say. When you take the
real Claret Jug back the following year, the R&A lets you buy a
replica for something like $6,000. Can you beat that? You win
their championship and they don't even give you a replica of
their trophy. Go figure that one out.

What's Your Favorite Movie?

I love *Godfather 1* and *2*. (Like everybody else, I hated *Godfather
3*.) I love all the *Rocky* movies. I love all the *Lethal Weapons*. I
love anything Clint Eastwood is in. My favorite golf movie is
Dead Solid Perfect with Randy Quaid. That movie is practically a
fucking documentary about the Tour. *Caddyshack* is hilarious,
but *Caddyshack II* was a disaster. *Tin Cup* is okay. *My Cousin Vinny*
is one of the funniest movies of all time.

You Play All Over the World. Got Any Travel Tips?

Yeah, I've done a lot of globe-trotting for a redneck Razorback from Dardanelle, Arkansas.

Australia I love, even though I've never played worth a shit there. And Germany I love, because my win at the BMW there in 2001 was my first win in six years and it kick-started my comeback.

The new stop on the European Tour, the Abu Dhabi Golf Championship in the United Arab Emirates, is great, too.

First, they've got a beautiful, beautiful golf course.

Second, the people are as nice as any I've ever met, just wonderful. And the place is all modern and immaculate. People say the Arab world is dangerous and scary, but Abu Dhabi sure isn't.

Third, the Emirates Palace may be the most luxurious hotel I've ever been in. They say it cost something like $3 billion. It's got to be one of the top hotels in the world. We were treated like kings. My suite was maybe 1,800 square feet. I asked them what it would cost if we were paying for it ourselves. Want to guess? Try $8,000 a night. It took me 19 hours to get there and 26 hours to get back because of kick-ass headwinds, but I'd go again in a heartbeat.

Do You Have Any Hobbies?

I'm a neat freak. I love to clean. I can't stand a messy house. I can't stand a messy bus. Hell, I can't stand a messy *anything*. And sometimes, because I'm me, I take it to extremes. My wife doesn't know how lucky she is.

What Else Do You Do When You're Home Besides Clean?

Usually I play with Little John for a couple of hours. We'll hit some golf balls together, and then go off to McDonald's or Burger King to get lunch. Then we'll come back and he'll go down for his nap. Then, depending on how I feel, I might drive down to Tunica to the casino. Or me and Sherrie might watch a couple of movies and eat some barbecue from A & R's. I work so hard when I'm on the road, either playing golf or working for my sponsors, that when I'm home I specialize in doing as little as possible.

What's Your Fondest Childhood Memory?

That's easy. When I was eight, I made it all the way down to the Punt, Pass & Kick regionals at the Superdome in 1974. Me and my mom and dad were on the elevator in the Dome, and the first person we see is Archie Manning. That was a huge thrill for me. I won, and then went to Washington, D.C., for the semifinal, where I got beat by a little Cowboys kid by about 2 or 3 inches.

What Was Your Childhood Ambition?

To make birdie and beat Jack Nicklaus by one stroke on the final hole to win the U.S. Open. Of course, I also loved football, baseball, basketball, soccer, and tennis—I played everything—and so I had my dreams about them, too. But golf was the hardest for me, at least at first, so that's what I went after. I can't tell you how many times I'd be practicing and say to myself—sometimes out loud, if nobody else was around—

"Okay, I got to make this chip to beat Jack to win this tournament." And then: "Yes! He made it!"

What's Your Favorite Restaurant in Memphis?

You mean besides Celebrities, which I own a piece of, and A & R Barbeque? Well, a couple of nights after Christmas, I took Sherrie to Ruth's Chris for a steak dinner. I like the meat, the bartenders know the brand of beer I drink, and it's only about 15 minutes from where I live. Plus, people around here are really nice. A few ask for autographs, but mostly they don't make a fuss and leave us in peace.

But usually I hate going out to dinner. I don't like to wait. I want to go in, eat, and get out. Nothing against fans or anything, it's just the way I've always been. That's why 90 percent of the non-home-cooked meals I've eaten in my life have come from drive-thrus.

But I got brownie points from my wife for that night at Ruth's Chris. It was the first time I'd taken her out to eat in a restaurant in about a year. We had a reservation for 7:00, but we didn't get there until 8:30. We were late because we were fighting over what was going to be in this book.

What Do You Think About Pro-Ams?

You're talking about a five-hour round, minimum, usually five-and-a-half. I'd rather spend one hour on the practice range and four hours relaxing back in the bus. Frankly, none of the guys on Tour really like the pro-ams. But pro-ams raise a shitload of money for the charities our tournaments support, and we're required to play in them by the Tour, so there's no point in bitching about them.

I try to make the best of them. Not for me, in terms of learning about the course or working on my game, but by helping the amateurs I'm paired with have a good time. I mean, these guys are paying a lot of money just to play a round of golf, and they're doing it for a good cause. My job, the way I see it, is to see that they have fun. Most of them are worried about embarrassing themselves, so I just try to get them to relax and remember that what they're doing beats hell out of working.

I don't volunteer golf tips or anything. The worst thing you can do to a guy who's already scared shitless about shanking one into the gallery is to tell him without being asked that his alignment is all fucked up. But if someone asks me something about his swing or how to play a shot, I'll give him my best advice, taking into account what kind of golfer he is.

Mostly, though, I try to get them involved in the competition, no matter what their games are like. That's the great thing about the handicap system in golf: with the right handicap, a guy who can't break 100 can kick the shit out of Phil Mickelson. I'm always saying things like, "Let's go kick some ass," trying to get everybody involved in winning. That's the point, after all. And it's damned sure the best way to have fun.

One of the big differences between pros and amateurs is how they react to a bad shot. A pro will do his best to forget about it and move on. Your average amateur will still be cussing himself out three holes later. So I try to keep guys from getting their dobbers down after they hit a bad shot. And if a guy has just made five or six horrible shots and only one or two decent ones on a hole, what I do is congratulate him on his good shot as we leave the green, and try to get him thinking about that and only that by the time we get to the next tee.

Sometimes it's hard, but usually I'm able to find something good in a guy's game to point out. You can't play golf if you go all negative on yourself, so I try my damndest to get my pro-am partners thinking positive.

You also have to be loose to play decent golf, so I clown around a little, get a little outrageous sometimes, whatever I have to do to get guys to loosen up. You can't believe how tense amateurs get playing in pro-ams. They're smart guys, usually, but somehow they get it in their heads that they've got to impress the pro they're playing with. Trust me, save your strength.

Four or five years ago, at the Sony Open in Hawaii, I got the best compliment I ever had from a pro-am partner. Our group was walking up the 18th fairway, and one of my teammates, a lean, athletic-looking guy with his hair in a ponytail like a hippie, comes over and starts walking beside me. He was the best golfer in the group (besides me, of course). Played to an eight or a nine, something like that. Probably could have been scratch if he played more, but he was CEO of an outfit called GameStop, a big-ass chain of video game stores that was spreading all over the country, and he didn't get to play all that much. Really sweet swing. Hit the ball a long way. Decent short game. So-so putter.

Anyway, he goes, "John, I've played in half a dozen pro-ams, and this has been far and away my most enjoyable experience." He thanked me for "keeping everybody in the game" and "showing genuine interest" in all his partners. He said some other shit, but by this time I'm too embarrassed and too tongue-tied to say anything.

It was nice, really nice, but I guess I'm not so good at

accepting personal compliments, maybe because deep down I'm not sure I deserve them. Also, I saw it as nothing special, just doing my job.

But I'd still rather be spending the time back in my bus, watching a movie and relaxing.

Music's a Big Deal in Your Life, Isn't It?

Life wouldn't hardly be worth living if it wasn't for music. Since I can remember, I've loved music, starting with the stuff my parents listened to: Perry Como, Burl Ives, Lawrence Welk on eight-tracks and TV. Then I moved on to country and southern rock. Ray Price, Jim Reeves, Merle Haggard. Waylon Jennings, Johnny Cash, George Jones. Willie Nelson, of course. Johnny Lee, he's one of my best friends now.

But shit, I liked it all, practically. Creedence and Lynyrd Skynyrd and Alabama and The Band. Dylan. I love Dylan. Hootie & the Blowfish. Stevie Ray Vaughan, all the good pickers. Buck Owens and Roy Clark on *Hee Haw*. Glen Campbell. Kris Kristofferson. Blues and R&B, too: Wilson Pickett, Percy Sledge, B.B. King.

And Elvis. Oh, hell, yes! There's an all-Elvis station on satellite radio that I listen to a lot. Some of his later stuff was shit, but the early stuff, it doesn't get any better.

I take my music with me wherever I go. I've downloaded a ton of CDs to my computer. And then the satellite radio has opened up a whole new world of stuff. I go to a foreign country, I don't understand a fucking word they're saying most of the time, but it's music, man. It's music.

I pick a little, usually when I'm on the road. That's another great thing about the bus, I know I can pick and sing and play my music pretty much as loud as I want to without bothering anybody or anybody yelling at me to turn it down.

But you can't do music in a half-assed way the way I do and get any good. I love it, but I'm not trying to fool myself that I'll ever be able to do anything more than fool around on the guitar.

What I do like to do, but only when something comes to me, is write lyrics. That's pretty much what I did in putting together my CD. I wrote down some stuff—I even wrote down one of my songs on a pizza box—and Johnny Lee and Darius and some of my other music friends who know what they're doing helped me find music to put it to.

More than anything, I wish I could make music like those guys.

Think You Have a Chance to Make the 2006 Ryder Cup Team?

Damned right I do. I believe in my heart I can play my way onto it. If I didn't, I shouldn't even bother teeing it up this year.

Playing on a Ryder Cup team is my biggest unfulfilled goal in golf, bigger even than winning a Masters. And I hope that if I do make a Ryder Cup team, this year or the next time, I can help change the nasty rivalry thing that's grown up in the last 15 years. I remember Fuzzy telling me how much things had changed. "Fuck, man," he said, "I used to go out drinking with these guys the night after we played. We were having a great time."

Then the Europeans started winning, and everything got really tense, really combative, like the other side was the enemy or something. The etiquette of golf went out the window at Ryder Cup time. Guys started saying nasty things about each other. Rather than cheering good shots, no matter who made them, the way they always used to do, fans started booing the other team. These guys from Europe are friends. I want to beat them every time I play them, sure. But I want to laugh and celebrate with them afterwards, too.

Really, this rivalry thing has gotten totally out of hand. The Ryder Cup got started as a friendly international competition. Now it's more like a world war.

As I said in a Q&A in *Golf Digest* last year, I'm not saying our guys don't like to have fun, and I'm not saying we all ought to go out and drink a bunch of beer. But I do think we need to loosen up. Both sides, but mainly ours, need to loosen up and have us some fun together.

Look, if I ever play on a Ryder Cup or a Presidents Cup team, I'd even wear a tie. I know there are a bunch of dinners you have to go to, and I can't stand wearing a tie. But I'd wear one for my country, even though I'd rather have a rope around my neck and be hanging from a tree.

Democrat or Republican?

I played golf with President Clinton twice—the first time was in Arkansas, when he was still Governor Clinton and was just learning the game; the other time was in Canada, when he'd learned the game well enough to say "mulligan" a lot. He was fun to play with.

I played golf with President Ford and Vice President Quayle at the Bob Hope Chrysler Classic in 1992 when I was so hungover I could barely stand up. They were good playing partners. And while I didn't make the cut, I did meet a future Mrs. John Daly.

I never played golf with President Bush Sr., but he and his wife, Barbara, always come out to see me when I play in Houston and give me a big hug. I know I'd like to play with him, because I hear he likes to play real fast.

I never played golf with President Bush Jr. either, but I did have the privilege of talking with him in the White House. In 2004, when I was in the D.C. area for the Kemper Open, I got word that he would like to meet me, and I jumped all over it.

Sherrie, Shynah, and Bud went with me, and when we were ushered into the Oval Office, I was like, wow, this is really it. We stand there a minute, and I'm nervous as hell, and then we see President Bush coming along the porch towards those glass doors on the other side of the room. He comes through the doors and walks over to us with that half smile on his face that he has, and he sticks out his hands and says, "Hiya, buddy! You still off the sauce?"

That broke the ice. We all laughed, and I introduced everybody, and we all shook hands. The president asked Bud what his connection was with me, and I piped up and said he's my agent. President Bush's eyebrows jumped up the way they do, and he cocks his head a little and says, "You've got a heckuva job there, Bud. You got any spare time? I think we could use a fellow like you around here."

(Don't think Buddy doesn't remind me of what President Bush said every time some problem comes up that I call on him to to deal with.)

Then we all sat down and shot the shit for a while. He asked Shynah about school. He congratulated me on winning in San Diego. And then he talked some about his golf game.

Someday, I hope to get to play with him. From what I hear, he's a better golfer than his dad but not as good as Clinton.

(In case you were wondering, I didn't wear a tie when I met President Bush. He wore one, and Bud wore one, but not me. As you may have heard, I hate ties.)

Mostly, although I've liked the politicians I've met personally, I'm not really into politics. If you want to know the truth, I think most of them only care about getting elected. Most of them tell you what you want to hear, then they do what they want to do.

The last two elections, I've been for Bush all the way. The Republicans, the way I see it, they finish the job. The Democrats, all they want to do is tax your ass off.

But as I said, I'm not really into politics.

Are You Going to Play on the Champions Tour?

For the answer to that, maybe you better talk to my godson, John Michael Sisinni, who knows his way around a golf course. John Michael's just 14, but he's been playing since he was 6, when his daddy took him to watch me play at the FedEx–St. Jude Classic in Memphis. He took lessons from a pro at 7 and won the first tournament he ever entered at 8—against kids ranging in age from 8 to 11. He was Mississippi State Champion in his age group at 9 and 11, and runner-up in Tennessee and Mississippi when he was 10. He finished fourth in his age bracket in the USJGA Tour Championship in 2005, which brought together the top 88 junior players in the country.

What I'm saying is that we may be talking about the 2015 Masters champion here in Mr. John Michael Sisinni.

Anyway, me and John Michael and his dad were sitting

around talking and he says to me, "JD, do you know who's going to be the greatest Champions Tour player of all time?" I say probably Tiger, if he wants to be. And John Michael says, "No, it's going to be you. They say that as you get older, your swing shortens some. That means by the time you're 50, your swing could be parallel."

Are You Ever Going to Stop Partying?

I could be a wiseass and tell you only when they pry that icy Miller Lite out of my cold, dead hand. Instead, let me tell you a couple of little stories. (Truth is, they amount to the same thing.)

Story number one took place one night a year or so ago, when my good friend John Sisinni—a top executive down at the Horseshoe Casino in Tunica—hired this big stretch limo and about 10 of us piled in and went out to paint the town. (Memphis, that is. Painting Tunica would mean just holing up in a casino, and that would get costly quick.)

We had some drinks at Celebrities, a nice bar that me and some friends own down on Beale Street. (Good music, good food, good prices—be sure to drop in whenever you're in Memphis. Tell them The Lion sent you.) And then we had us some fine Memphis barbecue, after which we had some beers at a couple of other places, and then we headed back to Celebrities, and . . . well, you get the picture. We were having us a fine old night on the town, and by one o'clock or so, none of us was feeling any pain.

Except me, that is. I was feeling pain in my chest. I thought I was having a heart attack. Fortunately, we were only about 10 minutes from Methodist Hospital in Memphis, and the limo driver made a beeline for it. Next thing I know, they've got me on a bed in this room with an IV in me and all I'm sure of is one thing: I ain't having no heart attack.

(It was gas or something, I guess—I never did find out.)

Matter of fact, I felt fine—a little drunk, but fine. Only I knew they weren't going to let me out until they ran a bunch of tests and shit, so I was going to be stuck there for a while.

That being the case, I call Sisinni in and ask him to do me a couple of favors. I ask him to bring me a cup of water, please, and he does. What he thinks I'm going to do, he told me later, is take some pills or something. What I do instead is fire up a Marlboro Light, using my cup of water as an ashtray.

The next thing I ask him to do is go out and bring back a Whopper with cheese and a double order of fries. There's a Burger King right close to the hospital, and it's been a while since the barbecue, and I don't know how long they're going to keep me tied down there.

So I'm covered until somebody comes around and tells me what I already know, namely, that I ain't having a heart attack. And pretty soon, the doctor does come in, only the first thing he tells me is to put out my cigarette at once. Don't I know this is a hospital?

Yes, I do know it, thank you very much.

And I also know that I've never ever before been ushered out of a hospital so fast—and without even having to get my stomach pumped.

Story number two took place last year, when I was down in Tunica investing some cash in the slots at the Horseshoe. A little after midnight, me and some friends went next door to the Sheraton to hear a little music and chill before heading home. We had a few beers and listened to this little C&W band play for a while, and we were just getting into the music when the waiter comes by and says the band stops playing at one o'clock. One o'clock? Shit, the evening's just getting off the ground, so I go up to the band and tell them I'll give them a thousand dollars an hour if they'll keep on playing. We finally left at 6 A.M., went and got us a sack of sausage biscuits at McDonald's, and headed on back home.

So back to the Q. Am I ever going to stop partying?

A: Not until they turn out the lights for good.

How's Your Musical Career Going?

Well, I've got a CD called *My Life*. I wrote some of the lyrics on the album, and some of my friends in the music business—Johnny Lee and Hootie & the Blowfish—helped me produce it. But the first time I ever got up and sang in public, at least when I was sober, was at the PGA Championship at Winged Foot in New York in 1997. I sang "Mustang Sally" with Hootie & the Blowfish in front of thousands of people. I was nervous, but everybody went crazy. Since then, I've sung and played a little guitar (always with real musicians covering my back) at my charity golf events in Arkansas and Memphis and other places. I usually do "Knockin' on Heaven's Door," which is also on my CD, because it's such a great song.

But as much as I love getting up in front of people and making an ass out of myself, I've got a family to feed, so I think I'd better stick with golf.

What Are You Going to Do Next?

Hell, I don't know. But I'll keep on keeping on. I don't like to live in the past, and I'm a little leery of predicting the future. I've done that too many times. By the time it finally gets here, all the future does is turn into the present and bite me on the ass.

○ ○ ○ ○ ○ ○

ELEVEN

STAND BY YOUR WOMAN

I always look on the bright side of things. I always think I'm going to hit a perfect shot. I always think I'm going to hit the next jackpot. And I always think that this time it's going to be love forever and evermore.

That's what I thought when I first laid eyes on Sherrie Miller. She was standing by the green on the 10th hole of the TPC at Southwind course during the first round of the FedEx–St. Jude Classic on June 7, 2001. She just flat blew me away. Man, she was beautiful. I said to myself—honest to God, I did, right then and there—I said, "I'm gonna marry that girl."

First, though, I had to meet her. Turns out that wasn't so hard. I walked up to her, introduced myself, and asked her if she would meet me in the parking lot after I finished my round. She said, sure, I'd like that.

I'll never forget what she said later when we got together: "I don't like blonds, and I don't particularly like golfers, but I do like fat boys."

Shit, I was a third of the way home.

Fifty-three days later, on July 29, 2001, we got married.

• • • • • • • • • • • • • •

You know, there must be something about me and 10th holes, because the first time I laid eyes on Paulette was on a 10th hole—at Bermuda Dunes during the 1992 Bob Hope Chrysler Classic. Funny, don't you think? Of course, that one didn't end up so funny.

Anyway, this time it was the first round at the FedEx, and I was coming up to the 10th green. The 10th at Southwind is 465-yard par 4, nothing tricky—a driver, sand wedge for me—nothing special. But this woman I saw standing next to the green, she was definitely special. I don't remember what I made on 10 that day, but I sure remember seeing Sherrie for the first time, and I remember asking her to meet me in the parking lot after the round.

Meanwhile, Leslie finally managed to show up near the end of the round—we only lived in a big house right there on the golf course—and she started crying because we'd been fighting. Just what I needed—here I am, trying to win a golf tournament, and my woman is standing around crying. Talk about a distraction. Hell, give me someone clicking a camera any day.

Guess I wasn't too bothered, though, because I almost won the tournament that week. It was me and Bob Estes, right down to the wire, Razorbacks versus Longhorns, the fans going nuts. People screaming "Ooooo, Pig! Soooie!" Hell, even a few hollering "Hook 'em, Horns!" But I made three bogeys on the back nine, and Bob hung tough. He won, and I finished T-5.

As I said, me and Sherrie met in the parking lot after the first round, and the minute we started talking, I fell absolutely in love with her, and I knew right then I had to break it off with Leslie. That next week, I went down to a casino in

Philadelphia, Mississippi. I had Leslie meet me there, and that's where I ended it with her. And I told her I was in love with Sherrie.

So that was it between me and Leslie. No marriage this time, so no divorce and no alimony. Just a shitload of gifts and stuff I'd given her, including the apartment and the car and the big-ass ring. And, naturally, the Rolex.

At the end, I don't even think there was much in the way of hard feelings between us. We'd had a real good time together, but we'd been fighting a lot recently, and we were probably both happy it was over.

At the time Sherrie and me met, she was working selling cars at her dad's automobile company. She was 25. I don't think any two people ever fell in love as quickly. Fifty-three days from how-do-you-do's to I-do's. That had to be some kind of record.

Just about all my friends were against us getting married. I don't know why for sure, but I think they were worried that somewhere down the road we would get a divorce or something. They thought it happened so fast, which it did. But you know what? I've been married to Sherrie longer than to any of my other wives.

Sherrie's very outgoing. She's got the same attitude towards the world that I do—namely, it is what it is. That means you just call it straight, don't be dancing around, just say what's on your mind. One night we were at a basketball game in Memphis, and these two kids sat in front of us in the box, only they were mostly standing up instead of sitting down. And Sherrie goes, "I can't see. Would you sit down? I don't want to look at your butts, I want to see the game."

That's Sherrie in a nutshell.

We got married in Vegas at the wedding chapel in Bally's

Hotel & Casino, where we were staying. Her mom came, and a couple of my friends were there, but it wasn't a big, splashy wedding. Sherrie was like 20 minutes late for us getting married because she wanted her dress just right. I've come to expect her to be late for everything.

She has a son by a previous relationship. That's one of the first things she told me when we met: "I have a one-year-old son. His name is Austin." I thought to myself, "Shit, I need a son." The first time I put him in my car, I had this big old McDonald's Diet Coke, and he stood up right there and reached over and started sucking on the straw, and I said to him, "Me and you are going to get along just fine."

And we do. Austin's seven now, and I love him like one of my own. Hell, he is one of my own. And now he has a little brother to play with, John Patrick Daly II, who was born on July 23, 2003.

Austin's a great kid. He loves Little John, and vice versa.

When I close my eyes and just listen to them playing together, I can see them growing up as a 21st-century version of me and Jamie, in terms of the strength of the ties that bind them.

··············

On July 28, 2003, five days after Little John was born, my father-in-law, Alvis Miller, my mother-in-law, Billie Miller, and my wife, Sherrie Miller Daly, were indicted by federal authorities on charges of laundering more than $1.2 million for an illegal drug and gambling operation. Over a year later, in October 2004, Alvis pled guilty to conspiracy to launder money and structuring of financial transactions to avoid federal reporting requirements; he was sentenced to two and a half years in prison. He's still in jail. Billie pled guilty to one count of structuring; she was sentenced to five months in prison. She served her time. Two months later, Sherrie pled guilty to one count of structuring; she was sentenced to five months in prison. She appealed the conviction, but her appeal was denied. This past January, while I was in California getting ready to play in the Buick Invitational, which I won in 2004, Sherrie went to jail to serve her five-month sentence.

This is the nightmare I've been living with for the past three years.

Sad thing is, with all this shit and confusion and stress, I don't really know a lot about this case. I just know that when the FBI comes down on somebody, it's never good news.

Evidently, all this came down as a result of a sting operation that had been going on for a while called Operation Dirty Pool. They ended up with about three dozen convictions. To me, only three of them mattered.

The FBI and the prosecutor said Alvis laundered money through his car dealership for a drug and gambling ring. Evidently, some of his so-called friends played let's-make-a-deal with the Feds.

The big drug dealer guy in this mess, I've known him for 15 years. I've played golf with him, and I for damned sure never knew he was running drugs from Mexico or wherever the hell it was coming from. I knew him probably just as well as Alvis did, and I never even so much as suspected he was running drugs and all that shit.

Knowing Alvis, who I call "Dad," I can't believe he knew these guys were involved with drugs. Alvis may have broken the law, but I know in my heart he wasn't messed up with drugs or drug dealing.

Billie Miller, Sherrie's mother—I call her "Mom"—spent five months in jail, though how you can put someone like her behind bars is beyond me. She's only one of the nicest people I've ever met in my life. I'm proud to be her son-in-law.

Looking back, I wish Sherrie hadn't appealed her conviction and had just done her time when her mother went away. It would all be over and done with, completely behind us, by now.

To tell the truth, I just want this shit to end.

················

After four shots at it, I think I've finally learned a couple of things about marriage. I know it's about sharing, but I also know—and so does my wife—that golf is a selfish, demanding profession. I'd like for my marriage to be a 50–50 proposition in terms of responsibilities, but I know it's not. I know it's more like 40–60—sometimes even worse than that—with Sherrie toting the heaviest load.

I just want Sherrie to understand that I'm doing what I'm doing for her and me and our kids. And she does understand but she doesn't understand, if you know what I mean. She understands that I have to be away from home a lot, in my case at least 35 weeks a year. But then when I'm home she'll say, Honey, when are we going on vacation? And I'll go, Baby, I *am* on vacation—I've been on the road, working my ass off, and now I'm not and I can relax and it's vacation to me.

Sherrie'll say, you've got to think of our family, and I do, honest I do. But she's got to understand just how big my family is. I've got my sponsors, and I owe them time. I've got my charities, and I owe them time. And I've got my fans, and I sure owe them time, because they're the ones who've always been there for me, who make everything else in my life possible.

Back in January, for example, a couple of days before I left for Abu Dhabi in the Middle East, I flew to Los Angeles to be on *The Tony Danza Show* to talk about *The Daly Planet*; then I flew to New York to be on *Conan O'Brien* to talk some more about *The Daly Planet* and do an interview for *The New York Times* food section; then flew to Orlando, where that night I autographed 1,250 8-x-10 photos for 84 Lumber, which was having a huge sales show the next day, where I sat and autographed stuff and gripped and grinned for seven straight hours; and then I flew to Pittsburgh, took a deep breath, and flew off to Abu Dhabi.

All this in less than 48 hours.

But I'm finally getting my shit together, and then this thing with Sherrie and her family knocks everything loose. Three of Sherrie's court appearances coincided with two Masters and a PGA Championship. Imagine trying to play a major while all that is going on?

On these court appearances, they want you there. Period. I've got to try and get ready to play this major, and I've also got to get the kids to day care. I've got to do this, do that, do some other thing. It's been tough on both of us.

But so many people have quit on me, so many have given up on me—including, sometimes, myself—that I know what it feels like, so I'm not quitting on her, I'm not giving up.

Me and Sherrie have been through hell in this marriage, but she guards me, she protects me. And I get pissed off at her, because she says what's on her mind, whether it's the CEO of a big company or anybody. She'll tell them just the way she feels. And that's fine if the other person is in the wrong. But sometimes she'll also get up in somebody's face when she's the one who's wrong, and she won't let it go. But as I said, she guards me, she protects me.

I've never loved a woman the way I love Sherrie. With Paulette, it was infatuation. With Bettye and Leslie, it was sex. With Dale, it was loneliness. With Sherrie, though, it's true love. Granted, we're always at each other's throats. I think me and Sherrie fight more than any couple in the world.

But it doesn't get in the way of the fact that I love Sherrie with all my heart and I always will.

So I'm hanging in there.

I'm not giving up on this family.

I love them too much.

Sherrie's the love of my life. I hope we'll stay together forever. We'll fight about stuff—we always have, so I guess we always will—but I think we'll stay together. I think this time it's love forever and evermore.

After all, me and Sherrie have a motto we've been living by:

We love each other just a little bit more than we hate each other.

TWELVE

○ ○ ○ ○ ○ ○

"WHERE I AM NOW"

That's the title of another song I wrote the lyrics for, and it seems like a good way to close out my front nine.

I turned 40 years old on April 28, and I'll be the first to admit it's been a hard 40. Fuzzy Zoeller, my best pal on the PGA Tour—actually, he plays on the Champions Tour now, which is fitting, because he's a true champion—used to joke that I wouldn't reach 50. At least I think he was joking.

No question about it, I've come close to the edge a lot of times. I've been my own worst enemy. But I think I've got a better handle on things now. I think I'm better off dealing with what's here, what's now, so that I'll be ready to deal with whatever tomorrow brings. After all, I've made it through the front side, but I know there are some pretty nasty hazards on the back side as well, and I better bring my A game.

The first of those hazards came into play this past January, of course, when Sherrie went off to jail.

The second hazard caught us in February when Austin's biological father, who'd never taken much of a role in his son's life, took advantage of Sherrie's felony conviction and incarceration to go to court and get temporary custody of Austin.

This like to broke my heart. I love Austin. I think of him as my son. He's part of my family. The fact that he's not being allowed to come out and stay with me on the bus from time to time, the way he's done over the past five years with his mom, is a real body blow. Based on my own feelings about being a dad, I can understand how a biological father might make a move like this. I just hope and pray that me and Sherrie will be able to do something about this situation. All I want is what's best for Austin.

What I know for sure is I can't let anger get control of me. I just have to accept this as something I have to deal with. I can't pretend I'm not deeply hurt and disappointed, but I know that letting anger boil over won't help matters at all.

The third hazard I have to overcome—and it's the most dangerous one of all—is my gambling.

················

Thirteen years ago, Hollywood Henderson warned me.

I met him at Sierra Tucson in January 1993, my first time in rehab, and after I got to know him a little bit, he told me, "John, you're going to find something that you're going to love to do as much as you loved to drink, and it's going to fulfill that part of your body that says, okay, I'm doing something. And you've got to be very, very careful what that is."

The people around me—my agents, my closest friends—were hoping, of course, that the "something" would be practicing golf.

No such luck.

What I found was gambling.

Gambling is the only thing that gets my juices flowing like golf does—or whiskey used to. As I told a writer for *Esquire* magazine about five years ago, playing slot machines for me is like being completely alone, on my own, like on a cross-country drive. All the noise in a casino? I don't hear it. I'm in a zone, and I'm all by myself. I'll check my watch, and maybe 10, 15 hours have gone by. It's scary how far away I get.

It's sort of like the way I felt when I was a teenager, and I'd be out on the golf course on a summer afternoon, when it wouldn't get dark until late. Everybody else had gone home, but I'd be there, all by myself, in this peaceful zone. I'd be totally locked in, working on my game, not thinking about anything or anybody else.

Out there on the golf course, with everything still and the day fading away, I was the only person in the world, and I felt good.

That's the feeling I get when I gamble.

And here's where that feeling got me in the 18 months after I left rehab in 1993: when I got to St. Andrews to play the 1995 British Open, I owed almost $4 million to casinos.

The only way I'd been able to keep my head above water was to turn all my quarterly endorsement income over to the casinos, and then run myself ragged by playing all over the world for appearance fees and by doing too many corporate outings, all because I needed the money to feed the beast.

The British Open saved me. Not because of the size of the winner's purse itself—it was only 125,000 pounds, which was like $200,000 back then. But after St. Andrews, when you throw in all my bonuses from my sponsors, I took a $1M+ haul away from the Old Course. All that went to the casinos. The rest of the summer and fall I spent collecting appearance fees at tournaments all over the world. By the end of 1995, when my quarterly sponsorship payments came in, I was able to pay off the casinos.

Then, in 1996, the whole cycle began again: up and down, back and forth, waiting for my quarterly checks to pay off the casinos, hustling appearance fees, running myself ragged doing corporate outings instead of spending time with my family and working on my game.

That's the way it's been for the last 10 years.

This worries me. A lot.

Sherrie has been very supportive on the gambling front. She tells me that the kids don't do without—and she's right about that. They all go to great private schools. They have everything they need. They're covered. They're set up just fine.

The problem is that if I don't get a grip on this thing now, what's going to happen as I get older and my earning power decreases?

I'll give you a perfect example of how destructive my gambling gets at times.

Last fall, after getting beat by Tiger in a playoff at the WGC AmEx Championship in San Francisco, I made $750,000 for finishing second, and generally felt pretty good about everything except my putting. I was real disappointed that I hadn't won, but at least I'd had a really nice payday.

But instead of going home and closing the 2005 PGA Tour season on a high note, I went straight to Vegas. My first stop was the new Wynn Las Vegas casino, where they have this $5,000 slot machine. Within an hour and a half, I was down $600,000. There went all that hard work against Tiger.

Next I went over to Bally's. Got a $600,000 line. Won about $175,000 and took it back over to that damned $5,000 machine. It owed me big-time. But I didn't hit shit on it. Got another $600,000 line from Wynn. Lost it in two hours on that $5,000 slot.

Back to Bally's, where I won another $80,000, then tried dialing down to the $100 slots, looking for a little streak so I could pay down some of what I owed.

No dice: in less than five *hours*, I lost $1.65 million.

So much for finishing the 2005 PGA Tour season on a high note.

And here's how my sick mind analyzed the situation: my sponsorship payments would be coming through in January, so I'd be able to pay everything off and get back to even by the beginning of the new year.

Everything's fine.

Everything's okay.

No problema.

Hell, yes, there's a *problema*. If I don't get control of my gambling, it's going to flat-out ruin me.

What burns me most, looking back, is that in the 12 years I've been gambling heavily, if I had left after the first hour and a half every time I was in a casino, I'd be up, *way* up. Instead, I'm down $50 to $60 million.

The fact is, 95 percent of the time that I go to a casino, the first 90 minutes I'm there I hit the biggest jackpots more often than anybody. I'm the luckiest guy on a slot machine you've ever seen—in the first hour and a half.

I like slots better than blackjack because of the solitude. It's just me, by myself, and I'm in total control. I just push the button and watch the machine. With the slots, it's like I'm driving my bus—I'm in control, just me.

Bud and Johnny, my agents, God bless 'em, they've busted their butts trying to throw a rope around me when it comes to gambling, but I haven't listened. And until I listen, the way I listened to my body with the medications and the whiskey, well . . . all I can say is that I'm just going to have to start listening soon, real soon.

Look, in balance, I've taken a lot more control of my life in the last five or six years. I'm off those damned medications. I don't drink JD anymore. I don't beat up on hotel rooms and cars as much.

Only gambling remains a problem.

So here's my plan. Every time I go to the casino, I start with the $25 slots. Plus, I set a walkout loss number. And the minute I hit that loss number, I quit, leave, just walk-the-hell-out. If I make a little bit, then maybe I move up to the $100 slots or the $500s, or maybe I take it to the blackjack table. It's their money. Why not give it a shot, try to double it? And if I make a *lot*, I can . . .

Well, that's my plan. It's a start. It's a start for *me*. I know, I know—I'm still a long way from quitting gambling.

What would I do if I did?

Drink?

That's not an option, at least in terms of whiskey. If I start drinking whiskey again, it'll kill me, plain and simple. I know that.

The only real option is to get control of my gambling.

················

A lot of stuff has come down on my head in the last five years. My father pulled a gun on me, my mother died, my best friend since first grade walked out on me, and my wife was convicted of a felony and sent to prison.

All that in five years.

Sometimes I feel like a character in a bad soap opera that's stuck in replay mode.

Sometimes I feel like getting in my bus and just driving away from it all.

And sometimes I feel like kicking my own fat butt for feeling sorry for myself. Everybody goes through tough times.

Everybody has troubles. Everybody has personal problems, family problems, relationship problems.

A long time ago, back in what I now think of as the "dark days," I was driving somewhere with Fuzzy Zoeller—probably looking for a bar—and I was bitching about something, how I was being screwed over by some wife or something. Suddenly he makes a left turn into this big graveyard and drives slowly into the middle of it, not saying a word. Finally, he pulls over, stops, turns off the engine, and turns to me.

"You think you have troubles, son?" Fuzz says. "Well, those folks in there are in a helluva lot worse shape than you are."

I know it.

I'm lucky: I was born with a special talent for hitting a little white ball and making people happy.

I'm blessed: I have four wonderful children who light up my life. I know just loving them is not enough, that I have to guide them and advise them and help them as they discover who they want to be. And I look forward to that challenge, although I suspect it will be the hardest one I'll ever have to face.

But I'm really and truly optimistic: I think I'm going to do even better on the back nine.

There are four big reasons for my optimism.

First, I have better control of my life now than at any other time since . . . well, in my life. My family life is rock solid. I have a wife I love to pieces, two great little boys at home with me, and two great young girls that I'm as proud of as any parent can be.

Plus, I don't think I have an alcohol problem anymore. As I joked one time to a reporter, I don't drink when I'm sober. I drink beer now, but I never drink whiskey. I honestly don't think I have a drinking problem anymore, and I don't think I ever was an alcoholic.

Second, I have a tight, solid inner circle of dedicated people around me, working their butts off on my behalf. My agents finally have me buying into their philosophy, which is for me to do what's best for me, and to stop being my own worst enemy. (It's only taken 15 years.)

Third, my financial house is in better order than it's been in a long, long while.

I have a good, solid group of first-class sponsors again, headed up by 84 Lumber, Hooters, Winn Grips, Mark Christopher Chevrolet, and, most recently, TaylorMade and Maxfli.

As of last fall, I'm the owner of Lion's Den Golf Club in Dardanelle, which I plan to turn into a dream place. I own a piece of a bar on Beale Street in Memphis called Celebrities. I've got John Daly's Discount Golf Shop in Russellville, Arkansas. (And I want to open one in Fayetteville and one in Memphis.)

Finally, John Daly Enterprises is getting off to a good start. I'm building a long-term strategic partnership on my Lion brand of apparel and other stuff.

All this means I don't have as many financial pressures as I did back when I was drinking—or later, when I was on all those antidepressants. That in turn means that I have a more solid foundation to stand on while I work to get control of the gambling. Plus, working to build and expand my businesses will, hopefully, keep my mind so occupied I won't be drawn to the casinos so much. That's the key: find something solid to replace what I found 13 years ago to replace whiskey.

The fourth big reason for my optimism about what lies ahead is that I'm playing good golf again.

My last two years on the golf course have been really solid: I jumped from nowhere on the World Golf Ranking in 2003 to 43rd in 2004, and I held on to that slot in 2005.

The move started even earlier when I won the BMW in 2001, my first win anywhere since the British Open in 1995, and then followed up in 2002 with a win at a tournament that Callaway puts on in Pebble Beach every year, and then a win in Korea in 2003. None of those three counted on the official PGA Tour money list, but the checks cleared, and when you've been through as long a dry spell as I had, it's nice to discover that you still know how to do it.

The most important win in my career, though, came at the Buick Invitational in 2004, when I knocked a long, tricky bunker shot to 7 inches for a tap-in birdie on the first playoff hole.

Biggest win? No, that would be the British Open in 1995.

But Buick was the most important because it breathed life back into my golf career. If you saw it on TV, you saw me bawling like a baby after I won. I was crying because this win proved to me and the world that I wasn't some washed-up has-been who'd drowned his talent in booze.

In 2004, I was named Comeback Player of the Year on the PGA Tour.

Last year, 2005, was almost as good. I didn't win, but I could have—twice, first against Vijay and then against Tiger— if I could have putted worth a shit. You go head-to-head in playoffs against the number one and number two players in the world, you know you belong, even if you lose.

This year, I've got my sights set even higher.

This year, I'm going to concentrate on becoming a grinder.

"Grinder" is a term you hear thrown around a lot in golf, but I'm not sure fans understand how we Tour guys use the term. I think fans may have the wrong idea that "grinder" means a boring golfer—a guy who makes few birdies and no eagles, does nothing splashy, takes no risks.

We define it a different way. To us, a grinder is a guy who doesn't give up, who keeps on keeping on, who plays hard and scratches for every par even when he doesn't have his A game. To us it's a term of high respect. On the Tour, it's a badge of honor to be thought of as a grinder, as a guy who never, ever quits trying.

So that's how I'm trying to deal with my gambling problem, by becoming a grinder, by grinding away at it, by not letting a setback or a loss throw me into a tailspin. I'm going to keep on working and working and working some more, and I'm not going to give up until I get it under control.

And while I'm grinding, I'm going to be guided by the advice my mother gave me a long time ago:

Champions come from the heart.

POSTSCRIPT

A while back, I went up to Nashville to talk to some music and theatrical agents about some projects I have in mind. We shot the shit about golf for a while, and then we talked about cutting a record, and then one of the guys asked me, "John, what else do you really want to do?"

"Two things," I told him. "Write a book and make a movie about my life."

The guy thought for a minute, and then he said, "Wait a while, John. You've got too much going on in your life to write a book or make a movie right now.

That was two years ago.

You're holding exactly the book I wanted to write.

I hope it helps you understand me better.

Now all I have to do is work hard and win another major, to give my movie a happy ending.

ACKNOWLEDGMENTS

A ton of FRIENDS have stood by me over the years without ever asking anything in return. There's been so many, I'm in a cold sweat right now for fear of forgetting somebody. Fortunately, they know who they are, and they all know I love them.

Top seed goes to my best friend, JAMIE DALY, who also happens to be my older brother. We've had us some times, Bro. *You* are Da Man!

Four dear people at Lion's Den Golf Club in Dardanelle saw an essentially abandoned blond-headed teenager who could hit a golf ball a country mile and took him under their wing: DANDY DON CLINE, JUDGE VAN TAYLOR, DICK BERRYMAN, and MRS. SHIRLEY WITHERELL, who on more Sunday afternoons than I can count let me ride shotgun on her golf cart so we could squeeze in 36 holes before dark. Thanks, all of you, for helping me grow up.

Old buddies BLAKE ALLISON (Yo, Bubba!), LANCE AWE, PETER VAN DER RIET, BRIAN VAN DER RIET, STEVE HOLDEN, DAN ROLLING, and the whole DARDANELLE GANG—throw me a beer, man—put up with a lot of shit from me over the years. And they gave back plenty in return. Then there's CHRIS LEGGIO, MARK and MARY ELLEN LEGGIO, and JAMISON BLAKE. Guys, you are my extended family, and I love you all.

New buddies—well, relatively new—JOHNNY LEE and JOHN SISINNI are the kind of guys you can call on anytime for anything for. I know. I've done it. And they've always, always delivered.

For 17 years, since before the 1991 PGA Championship, BUD MARTIN and JOHN MASCATELLO have represented me, but to identify them as "agents" doesn't begin to suggest what they've done for me and what they mean to me. Along with TERRY REILLY, they've rescued me from one jam after another over the years more times than I can count—and certainly more times than anyone in his right mind could have expected them to.

They've counseled me, cheered for me, lifted my spirits, and—when I've needed it, which has been often—kicked me in the butt. They've shown me the right path, told me when I took the wrong one, and helped me mature (at least some). They've tolerated a whole lot of intolerable behavior on my part, and paid it back with a ton of tough love.

GLEN WAGGONER has written three golf books; a ton of magazine articles for *Esquire, Men's Journal*, and other magazines; and *Rotisserie League Baseball*, the book that introduced the fantasy sports game which he and a bunch of his cronies invented 25 years ago. (It's even spread to golf.) He was one of the founding editors of *ESPN The Magazine*, and he's currently the executive editor of ESPN Books. But his greatest challenge in sports journalism was translating my recollections, rants, and raucous ramblings into passable English. If he pulled it off—and you'll be the judge of that—it's probably because he hails originally from Texas. Or, as we like to call it back home, Southwestern Arkansas.

HarperCollins senior vice president and executive editor DAVID HIRSHEY took a big risk on a golfer who hasn't read a book cover to cover since *The Grapes of Wrath* in high school. Maybe he'd heard that I was a 66-to-1 long shot going into the 1995 British Open. Thanks for having faith. Thanks as well to David's editorial caddies, MILES DOYLE and NICK TRAUTWEIN, for getting all the yardages right and keeping me out of hazards. And a tip of the visor to researcher LINDA WESLEY, who did her dead-solid best to make sure I didn't sign an incorrect scorecard.

Thanks also to my literary agent, SCOTT WAXMAN, who sang my praises in words that New York publishers could understand.

More than just my most loyal sponsor, JOE HARDY, the visionary leader of 84 Lumber, has been like a father to me. Thanks for everything, Dad. So I guess that makes MAGGIE HARDY MAGERKO a younger, smarter, wiser sister. Thanks for everything, Sis.

Two wonderful, generous people—LYNETTE and BOB HOLMES—offered me their strong shoulders to lean on after the death of my mom. Guys, I can never thank you enough for the unconditional love you have given me.

KEN GARLAND built my all-time favorite home for me. Together with his wife, MARGARET GARLAND, we have built one of the all-time great friendships. You're two of the big reasons I love Memphis.

We try to beat each other's brains out, but the guys on the PGA TOUR really are one big brotherhood. Through all my struggles, I've always received love and support and understanding from just about everybody I've teed it up with. Early on, there was my mentor and partner in crime, Mr. FUZZY ZOELLER. You taught me a lot, Fuzz, and some of it didn't even get me into trouble. Guys like CRAIG STADLER and HUBERT GREEN made a young, long-haired punk feel like he belonged, even when he wasn't so sure himself. Along the way, PETER JACOBSEN and COREY PAVIN and BOB ESTES and MARK BROOKS and JIMMY McGOVERN (and the list goes on and on) went out of their way to give me a boost when I needed one. More recently, PAT PEREZ and TIM HERRON have shared plenty of laughs with me. And whenever I was in trouble in the last 15 years, superstars like TOM WATSON and ARNOLD PALMER and GREG NORMAN were always among the first to call me and tell me to hang in there.

Finally, where would I be today without the inspiration and example of my childhood idol, JACK NICKLAUS? Thanks, Jack, for your many words of support and encouragement over the years.